D0372160

Refresh!

Having Transformed Thoughts and Lives

"...so that times of refreshing
may come from
the presence of the Lord,"
Acts 3:19

Sue Boldt

Refresh!

Cover Photo: Lightstock.com – Geoff Duncan
Author Photo: Jeremy Boldt – Luna Studios, Portland, OR

Cover Design: Randy Boldt

ISBN: 10:1497539544
ISBN-13: 9781497539549

DEDICATION

To my husband, Randy,

who loved me with the love of the Lord Jesus
in spite of and through
my darkest hours,
and still loves me lavishly
as we walk in God's light and truth together.

CONTENTS

ACKNOWLEDGMENTS

Much credit is due to the women who came along side me to act as editors for this book. Rachel Lobo, Julie Thomas, and Jaime Betters not only tried to capture stray commas and difficult to understand sentences, they became my biggest cheerleaders along with my husband, Randy. They captured my passion for seeing men and women find wholeness in Jesus and made it their passion, as well. I cannot thank them enough for taking countless hours away from their incredibly busy schedules, families, and lives. Any boo-boos are because I did not take their advice at times.

This book might never have been written without the encouragement of Rachel Key and the women who attended the *Refresh Conference* held at *The Highlands Christian Fellowship*, Palmdale, CA. The Lord used this particular event as the impetus to put my thoughts...regarding our thoughts, on paper.

A big thanks to Lisa Greer (mostly for being...Lisa Greer!), for providing the title over dinner at the Cheesecake Factory.

Above all, I thank the Lord Jesus Christ for His lavish and unfailing love. He *refreshes* my everyday life with His presence, He sees my heart and is *restoring* it, and He touches my wayward thoughts to *renew* my mind. To Him be all glory...

# Introduction

Refresh! Restore! Renew!

I just really like these words. No, I really *love* these words.

I'm a beach girl at heart. Having spent all my youth until marriage within a mile's distance of the beautiful southern California coastline, nothing speaks to me of cleansing, effervescence, jubilation, recovery, new beginnings, hope, and effusive joy like the sight and sound of radiant blue surf. Okay…it does not take much to get me excited!

When I think of *refreshing*, *restoration*, and *renewal*, I'm also reminded of the *rivers of living water* that Jesus spoke about when describing the work of the Holy Spirit in a believer's life. Hmmmm…all of the mighty rivers I have ever viewed, jumped in, or rafted upon seem to bubble up and over, dance with delight, and exude refreshment with every watery spray. They are also mighty enough to move boulders, logs, and any other obstacles hindering their path. I most definitely feel and experience the strength of the river's current. Again, it does not take much to get me excited.

Possibly my attachment to these important words, found so often in the Bible, is due to the fact that I lacked the *experience* of them for a period of time in my life when I desperately needed them. Though my circumstances were quite wonderful ~ beautiful children, loving and amazing husband, comfy home, and successful ministry ~ my thought-life was under siege and out-of-control. Consequently I felt almost everything that is the antithesis of these three marvelous words. I was discouraged, lifeless, and weary.

Since my early teenage years when I first fell in love with the Lord Jesus Christ and the power of His gospel, I had drifted somewhere in my heart. Mind you, I was a Christian who was fairly comfortable in praying for people and "moving" occasionally in the gifts of the Holy Spirit. Somewhere along the way, however, while trying to find significance in my busy everyday life as a young mom and pastor's wife, I had placed super-human expectations on myself that I could only realize by fantasizing about them.

Try as hard as I might, I couldn't control my thoughts. In the wake of this addiction (for that is what it was) I developed a full-blown eating disorder. Needless to say, this entire struggle did not make me a "happy-camper." Depression soon came knocking on my door, and I had little strength to resist it. My heart needed mending from all of the damage I had allowed our adversary, the devil, to do.

Oh, but for the Lord of *refreshing*, *restoration*, and *renewal*! Jesus had never left my side, and the power of His Holy Spirit still resided in me. He never gave up on me – even when I lost my *first love* and seemed to tumble out of His embrace. He is here for you, too.

You may not have an issue with daydreaming, an eating disorder, or depression like I did, but we all have life areas we would love the Lord to touch. We need daily *refreshing* instead of the daily grind; victorious *restoration* of what the world and the devil have stolen from us; and continual *renewal* into the image of Jesus instead of rehashing our same flaws and failures.

We may struggle with anger, guilt, unforgiveness, fears, bad habits and behaviors, our views of ourselves and others, addictions, hang-ups, deep wounds, or worry...the list could go on and on. As Christians we have the hope of heaven, but what about hope for the life we lead here on earth?

According to God's Word, the Bible, our minds and our hearts have a whole lot to do with the way we live. Duh! Kind of a no-brainer there! Some food for thought, however. If our hearts and minds could be renewed by the Lord of love, and if we began to take even baby steps in what the Apostle Paul describes as *walking in the Spirit*, possibly our actions would be transformed more into His glorious image. Wow! I'd like some of that action!

This booklet isn't a formula to follow (has Jesus ever done anything the same way twice?), nor is it a self-help book (has trying to fix ourselves ever worked?). This book is simply *one* way of looking at our thought-lives through the Scriptures that has benefited a few others and myself.

I highly encourage you to read the passages we'll be studying slowly. Be sure to underline or highlight the Bible verses the Holy Spirit seems to be speaking directly to you. When we take a look at the original Greek language of some of the word translations, it will also help if you underline the words or phrases that mean most to you. You will be greatly enriched by doing this.

I pray the Holy Spirit will use the words of this book to encourage you to passionately pursue Jesus and His wholeness for your life – most particularly in the arena of your mind and heart.

Are you ready to dive and dance in the Lord's waves and leap into His life-giving river? Could you use some *refreshing, restoration,* and *renewal*? I sure could and I want more and more!

What are we waiting for… let's get going!

Love,
Sue Bee

Refresh!

One Saturday Morning

*"He sent from above, He took me; He drew me out
of many waters.*
  He delivered me from my strong enemy,
*From those who hated me, For they were too strong
 for me. ...*
  He also brought me out into a broad place;
He delivered me because He delighted in me."
Psalms 18:16-17, 19

I was a mess.

One Saturday morning just shy of my 35th birthday found me on
my knees in a time of private prayer with the Lord. The house was
quiet while my husband, Randy, and our three kids were peacefully
sleeping-in before a round of little league and girls' softball games
began later that day.

Seeking to grab a few minutes with Jesus and His Word would be
a great comfort to me this day; that is, if I would be able to keep my
thoughts focused on Him for any length of time. For the first time in
about eighteen months, in the midst of a mild to moderate depression,
I'd had a bit of hope light-up my heart a few weeks earlier. Of all

things, while reading an old Christian novel, "The Robe," the Lord had melted my heart enough to help me remember that all things are possible with Him. A fresh surrender to Him had ensued. This particular Saturday I sought to meet with Him and hear His voice.

On the "outside" I led an enviable life. Truly. Though five years earlier I had announced to my husband I no longer loved him and wanted out of our marriage – we were now in a stable, loving, and good place with each other. Our two daughters and our son were bright, darling, healthy, and full of life. The home we shared was our first as homeowners – in a nice neighborhood in a lovely city. The church we had "pioneered" eight years earlier continued to blossom, by God's grace, under our young leadership. Yet, with all of the great externals of my life, I now found myself with a black cloud over my head daily. I was weepy, unsatisfied, moody, discouraged, and depressed.

Sunday School lessons about the Lord Jesus had touched my heart at an early age. I was the only, greatly loved, child of church-going parents. My dear, sweet mom had always loved the Lord; in the particular tradition she had been raised, though, she knew the love of God but not of His power in her personal life. As a young girl I believed that Jesus loved me, had died and risen for me, and my faith in Him had brought me into right standing with God. However, that is about all I knew... until I was fourteen years old and a Holy Spirit-filled singing group came to visit my staid Lutheran Church youth group and rocked my world!

At the height of the Jesus Movement in the early 1970's, I experienced the baptism in the Holy Spirit on my own. This new found reality of a personal relationship with Jesus Christ profoundly changed my life and the direction I had been heading. At the wonderful age of sixteen, I met my amazing husband who was gifted musically and traveling the country in a Christian country-rock band.

Though music was his passion, Randy sensed the Lord calling him to pastoral ministry and I was in full agreement. We married a year after finishing high school; started raising three wonderful children, and by our mid-twenties, realized our dream of pastoring a growing church body.

With all of these wonderful gifts God had graced me with – marriage, family, and church – I still became horribly entangled in some pretty severe and debilitating behaviors from which I was powerless to break free. The depression I had been experiencing was the capstone to years of engaging in bulimia, an eating-disorder that consumed my every thought and almost every activity I participated in. When my appearance wasn't at the forefront of my mind, I succumbed to a numbing fantasy life where I could be, quite literally, the person of my dreams: beautiful, witty, wise, adorable, and smart. In my daydreams I was God's gift to Christianity and to the world at large. Certainly in my dreams I was the perfect woman, wife, mother, and Christian!

Finally, when having intimacy with my husband, my thoughts turned to sexual fantasy. Enough said.

I loved Jesus with all of my heart, but somewhere in the brokenness of my heart and mind it seemed like I had lost my way, even though I was still reading His Word and even teaching it! I still had quiet times with my Lord, but I struggled to keep my mind focused on what I was doing. I sensed and had seen the work of the Holy Spirit innumerable times throughout my life – powerful moments with Him alone and corporately with other believers during services, retreats, and special events. Yet, I didn't know how to maintain His presence in my daily life. My life struggles were like huge boulders in my path to moving forward in Him. I felt bucketsful, no, oceans-full of guilt.

At the time of our marriage crisis five years prior to that wonder-filled Saturday morning, I had come to my husband's office at the church and told him I no longer loved him and wanted out of our marriage. I walked out on him *and* our children later that evening. By the absolute grace and hand of the Lord Jesus alone, I returned a few hours later when I realized leaving Randy and our children would mean exiting my walk with Him.

How I thank the Lord for His mercy to cause me to return home and give our marriage a second chance! Later, two of our best friends left their wives and families, and lost their pastoral ministries reciting the same words to their spouses as I had said to mine – except they *did not* return home. Yes, God's grace has extended to their lives; He never gives up on us and always calls us to His embrace, nevertheless, they have paid a terribly high price for their decisions.

Ironically, to my way of thinking (which was skewed at best!), the Lord used my walk-out experience to cause Randy to invite the Great Counselor, the Holy Spirit,[1] to search his own heart and receive deep healing. In an instant Randy was changed. I sensed it the moment I walked back into our home The "atmosphere" was different.

Randy's need to "control" me was broken. He had made the decision to release me to the Lord, and he also made the conscious choice to follow Jesus no matter what *I* did. God honored his surrender, and the enemy's grip on this area in Randy's life was annihilated.[2] Just sensing the transformation in him compelled me to stay in the marriage, family, and ministry, though my thought life was far from being sound and stable.

Indeed, though I was s-l-o-w-l-y walking with Jesus out of the physical symptoms of the eating disorder, my thoughts were still consumed by my appearance. The "dailyness" of life, church issues, and a sense of insignificance, which led to unhealthy expectations I had of myself and our ministry, only drove me deeper into a daydream world where everything was perfect…namely me!

However, that Saturday morning I came to kneel at the Lord's feet and open His Word. There, He met me.

I have come to believe He is *always* ready to meet us…indeed He is closer than our breath at all times. Most of us don't give real credence to the fact that His every thought is directed towards us – intentionally and incessantly, beyond what we can comprehend.[3] Our God is a consuming fire; He is jealous for us to know that – with all our flaws, failures, and brokenness – we are individually all He thinks about.[4] His love is ever released and lavished in our direction, waiting to be received by us.[5] But head knowledge needs to become heart knowledge, and theory must become experience.

As we journey through the pages of this book, I'll unpack more of what I have learned from my own story that may be of help. I hope to spare you some of the detours I took, which may have delayed His hand to restore me. At the end of this book are several other brief, true-life stories to encourage you as well. Jesus almost never seems to do things the same way twice, so this is *not* a formula for freedom, by any means. However, I pray what is shared is an encouragement for you to seek the Lord to see how He wants to breathe *refreshing*, *restoration*, and *renewal* into your personal situation.

Back to the story…

I was kneeling on our living room carpet. My Bible lay beside me. I didn't journal then like I do now, so I don't quite remember the sequence of events, however, somewhere in the midst of praying I reached for a Christian magazine that was on the coffee table. A little strange, don't you think? (Again, no formulas to try and emulate!) I turned to an article I had not read before.

This article, written by John Dawson, related how he had led a Youth with a Mission (YWAM) team to Rio de Janeiro, Brazil, to preach the gospel. This team had not found any success reaching the upper echelons of society and the business world while sharing daily in the financial district of the city. Discouraged and dismayed, the team met together for prayer in a plaza at the center of the district. The Holy Spirit prompted them to war spiritually against a *spirit of pride* that oppressed the region. However first, they had to relinquish their *own* personal issues with pride. They knelt down by a beautiful fountain in the middle of the square and confessed their sin. The Spirit moved. All around them men in high-priced business suits fell to their knees. Women in stilettos and carrying briefcases, scurrying to their next appointments, fell to their faces, sobbing, seeking salvation from the Savior.

That Saturday morning, the Spirit moved in me too. I "saw" that I had allowed a demonic *spirit of pride* to take up residence in my heart and mind (much more about this later!). I had thought my issue was rooted in worthlessness, not pride! Didn't I despise the way I was? Didn't I have a low self-esteem? You could have hit me over the head, and I would not have believed that the root of my issues was *pride*.

I now realize that pride and shame usually walk hand-in-hand. Shame is at the core of most of our lives, however, to compensate for shame, it is human nature to *prove* we are *better* than who we really think we are. In that combustible combination, pride happens. This is the enemy's ploy and he (the devil) does not play fair.[6] This is a pretty simplistic explanation, and I certainly didn't see all of this at that time. All I knew that Saturday morning is the Holy Spirit was diving deep into me, unlocking the stronghold of pride that lay at the root of my obsession with appearance, insignificance, and dissatisfaction with my life.

With tears and sobs of my own, I confessed my sin of pride. I don't remember my exact words, but I renounced everything having to do with pride. Something left me. That is all I knew. I didn't know much about spiritual warfare, but it didn't matter. Tears are in my eyes, even now, remembering the graciousness of my God to come and rescue me. He is something else…

We are not to base our faith on our feelings, but let me tell you, the Holy Spirit flooded my being and I sure felt it! I experienced waves upon waves of release and freedom, love and exhilaration, purpose and hope! I felt a river of living water welling up inside like I had experienced many times earlier, however, there had been such a drought for many recent years.

It was truly like the floodgates of heaven had opened. Throughout that week the Lord lavishly gifted me with several "yes" answers to prayers I had long prayed. I experienced a miraculous healing to a chronic physical condition from my youth. I actually became ill from the medication I had taken for years for this condition, and the Lord spoke to my heart to stop taking it because I was healed – and it was true! I have never taken that medication again, nor have I ever again experienced that chronic condition. More importantly, I have never had a bout with depression…ever…again.

> *"Therefore if the Son makes you free, you shall be free indeed."*
> John 8:36

Progressing Forward…

Now for a reality check.

Have I ever been tempted to be depressed? Yes, but rarely. Kind of like a glancing touch on the shoulder, coming from the *outside* of me rather than the *inside* of me. However, I have found it easy to not give place to it, even in my darkest hour – why would I want to go back to that blackened dungeon?

Have I ever been discouraged? A definite yes! Nevertheless, discouragement is not depression, and there is a difference. I think of depression as a continual dripping of despair over myself, my circumstances, or my future. Discouragement has more to do with set-backs, unpleasant situations, or disarmingly bad news *for a season.*

On that Saturday morning was I set free from my eating disorder? No, not completely. However, a key had turned in the lock of that stronghold. Appearance is often rooted in pride/shame. In much the same way Israel took the Promised Land, I won some battles and lost some battles. I'd move five-steps forward and then slide three-steps backward. I would progress four-steps forward, then fall six-steps backward. Still, I was gaining ground. The Lord spoke to me out of Psalm 144:1-2:

> *"Blessed be the LORD my Rock, Who trains my hands*
> *for war, And my fingers for battle—*
> *My lovingkindness and my fortress, My high tower and*
> *my deliverer, My shield and the One in whom I take*
> *refuge, Who subdues my people under me."*

From this passage I learned that I was to get my daily marching orders from Him as to how to proceed with my eating – a "battle-plan" for the day. This caused me to be utterly dependent on the Lord, and I began to hone my skills at hearing His voice.

I have likened this particular aspect of my journey in freedom to having worn, as it were, a yucky, ugly, dirty, tattered robe while walking along a path. As the Lord Jesus walked with me on this path and I progressed a few steps forward then a few steps backward, He was always a bit ahead of me, but close enough to touch. He waited patiently when I was in back-track mode, nevertheless, He always kept extending His hand to me to inch forward.

It was precisely five years later when I was absolutely, irrevocably freed from the grip of this disorder and its entanglement with my mind and body. The final blow was delivered without my being aware of it during a time when our family was making a huge relocation to another part of the state that consumed all my thoughts, prayers, and energy. That old robe had fallen off of me somewhere on the path behind me. I could see it on the ground way back in the distance, however, I was too far from it to ever put it back on…Hallelujah!

Since that day, I have not obsessed about food, weight or my appearance. I eat what I like, when I like, but rarely eat past the sense of first fullness. I don't weigh myself, yet I wear a sensible size in clothing for my frame and height. I write this to encourage you that the Lord desires to heal and free you completely; not just provide a means for you to *cope* with life issues. This applies to whatever addiction or stronghold (something that has a strong hold on you!) that you may be experiencing.

Now, back to that Saturday morning and my thought life – for this is the greater part of the substance of this book…

Was I immediately free from my daydream world? Yes, I believe I was set free in that moment. However, I didn't know how to **walk** in my freedom. For three months following that Saturday morning, my thoughts were clear from living in a fantasy world of my making. Yet, slowly, these thoughts crept back. Not all of the time, but often enough to distract me from the Lord and all He wanted to do in my life. These nearly life-long thought patterns had become well-worn ruts that were easy for me to fall into. Especially when I had moments of great joy or sadness, or when in crowds and I was tempted to feel insignificant. Music would often be a trigger – how like the devil to tempt me with what he had once been master of before his great fall from God's presence.[7]

The same held true for me regarding sexual fantasy during intimacy. I was free, but the go-to places in my mind were easy to resort to. With the Holy Spirit in charge, He enabled me to intentionally re-write these scripts.[8] God's intended beauty during intercourse slowly became a heart-reality and a life-reality for me.

No, I was not depressed – but I stumbled and fell a lot. Sometimes it seemed like I was *down* longer than I was standing upright. Yet I was moving forward, even when it seemed that I had stalled on the Lord's victorious path for me.[9] When guilt wanted to reign supreme, the Lord's lavish grace abounded.[10]

Ultimately, total and complete release, absolute freedom, and the ability to continue to walk in liberty came from experiencing *times of refreshing from the presence of the Lord*.[11] This does not mean I am not tempted in this old area at times; it means *the struggle is over*. It is no longer a constant wrestling match with the enemy of my soul or with my flesh to see who is going to get the upper-hand. The enemy and my flesh may attempt to distract me at times, however, God's presence is simply sweeter, richer, and more glorious than their sickly invitations. Standing in the truth of God's Word and having a better understanding of who I am in Christ sends temptations packing. Why would I want to go back to the dark pit I once lived in?

Choosing to make living in His presence and having the truth of His Word in my heart the *sole purpose* of my life has made all the difference.[12] I had no clue how satisfying my life could be…and I'm just beginning this journey, even now! It turns out that Jesus wants this more for me more than I do, and He has been so patient with me as I learn! This journey with Jesus is what this book is about...

As you have read, I seem to have a "bump down the hallway" or a "stub-your-toe-often" method of walking with Jesus. I don't think it is necessarily what God's Word (the Bible) *always* prescribes for receiving His guidance for your life; still, it seems to be how the Holy Spirit is able to communicate with my stubborn mind and heart.

To further explain what I mean, it's as if I can "see" the purpose or the destination the Lord Jesus has in His mind for an area of my life, but I can't seem to get there in one straight line. Rather, it's like I'm walking down a long hallway. I tend to continually veer to the right or left trying to figure out whether using the doors that appear on either side might be a quicker, easier, or more efficient way of getting to where He is wanting me to go.

I *am* moving forward, but I easily get stalled, trying one way of doing things until the Holy Spirit gently tells me that the particular door I'm trying to open isn't exactly what He meant. He then moves me back into the corridor of the hallway. All the time, even when it seems I have parked myself in some door jam, the Spirit is teaching me – what to do or not do. I am taking ground. I am moving forward. I am learning to possess my possessions in Him.[13] Namely my freedom from areas of my life and thoughts that have held me captive. And, when I gain hard-fought ground, I *am* less tempted to give it back to my enemy again. The Lord is able to "milk" all of my experiences for my good, even the really terrible ones...hey, isn't that a famous scripture somewhere? Romans 8:28-29 to be exact.

Apparently the children of Israel had this same learning experience when overcoming their enemies and taking hold of their Promised Land:

*"And the LORD your God will drive out those nations before you **little by little**; you will be unable to destroy them at once, **lest the beasts of the field become too numerous for you**.*

"But the LORD your God will deliver them over to you, and will inflict defeat upon them until they are destroyed."

Deuteronomy 7:22-23

I pray that you can learn from my experience how the authority of God's Word and the *refreshing*, *restoring*, and *renewing*, power of His presence can lead to greater freedom for your own life. I also pray that you will be spared some unnecessary detours that might hinder your progress as you read how I bumped down the hallway from the grip of my own brokenness, the seduction of the world, and the snares of our adversary. Most of all I want to encourage you that God is faithful, He is powerful, He loves you completely and totally. He is on your side and wants to set you free from areas of your life that are less than all that He has for you in Christ.

Jesus is extending His hand to you...Will you accept His invitation?

"He also brought me out into a broad place; He delivered me because He delighted in me."

Psalms 18:19

Study Questions...

- Though you may have experienced different struggles than mine, can you identify with anything from this chapter? Explain.

- What are you own personal issues that need a personal healing touch from the Lord Jesus? (Share only if comfortable if you are in a group study.)

- Did this chapter raise any questions for you? What are they?

- If you received any encouragement from this chapter. What was it?

- Reread the opening verses from Psalm 18 at the beginning of this chapter. What is the Holy Spirit saying to your heart?

---

[1] John 15:26

[2] 1 John 3:8

[3] Psalm 139:18, Jeremiah 29:11

[4] Deuteronomy 4:24

[5] Jeremiah 31:3

[6] 1 Peter 5:8

[7] Ezekiel 28

[8] Romans 12:1-2, 2 Corinthians 10:3-5

[9] Psalm 37:24

[10] Romans 8:1

[11] Psalm 16:11, Acts 3:19

[12] Matthew 6:33

[13] Obadiah 1:17

A Little Homework - Christianity 101

"A PSALM OF DAVID.
*He makes me lie down in green pastures, He leads
me beside quiet waters,*

*He **refreshes (restores) my soul**. He guides me along
the right paths for His name's sake."*
Psalm 23:1-3 NIV *(restores*: NKJV)

Wow! The Lord is my shepherd...I lack nothing!

That phrase alone from this beloved psalm pretty much sums up
our walk with Jesus. He *is* our good Shepherd who laid down His life[1]
for His wayward lambs, and in Him we find everything we need to
navigate life here on planet Earth.[2] Quite simply, He is more than
enough.

The word Jesus uses in the New Testament about life found in
Him is that it is *abundant*.[3]

'*...I have come that they may have life, and that they
may have it more abundantly."*
John 10:10b

19

The original Greek New Testament definition of the word *abundant* leaves no doubt of the Lord's intent for His followers:

Perissos Greek – Meaning: Superabundance, excessive, overflowing, surplus, over and above, more than enough, profuse, extraordinary, above the ordinary, more than sufficient.

No, this has little to do with our circumstances, position, bank account or toys in the garage – though He generously blesses His kids. This has way more to do with His lavishness to bring overflowing abundance to our lives *no matter what we are facing*.[4] Even in the presence of our enemies (any difficult circumstance thrown at us by the world, the devil, or our own failings), Jesus serves us a feast. No skimpy peanut butter and jelly sandwiches for us! He gives us a sit down, can't eat enough, over the top "meal" in the excessive sense of His presence which is more than enough to satisfy us from within. King David continues in Psalm 23, "My cup runs over!" Yet why is it we live so many of our days in a "less than" mode?

If we are truly going to find help in seeing our thought lives, and consequentially, our daily lives continually transformed into the image of Jesus, we need a little Christianity 101...some Bible basics. What does David mean in his psalm that his *soul* is *refreshed* and *restored*? Do David's words have any bearing on *the way we think*?

When I was in school, I was a pretty good student, however, I was never too excited about the homework. Nevertheless, if I didn't understand the basics of a subject, I couldn't move forward in exploring the exciting material my teachers *really* wanted me to learn. It would be like building a house without a secure foundation.

First Things First...

First of all we need to recognize that our transformation into

Christ's image will be our life-long pursuit. This marvelous journey of faith will have mountaintops and valleys, smooth sailing and rough waters, but the Lord assures us He will never leave our side and His Holy Spirit will be at work in us, through us, and all around us.[5]

As we cling to Jesus, we'll not only have all we need to face any circumstance, but He will be transforming us from the inside out into His likeness. The world around us will take notice that we are His children and they will then want this extraordinary life that we have in Him.[6] I'm certainly not where I want to be walking in this weary world as His image-bearer – I've got a million miles to go – but by His grace, I've come a long way baby!

> *"Love has been perfected among us in this: that we may have boldness in the day of judgment;* ***because as He is, so are we in this world.***"
> 1 John 4:17

It is the Lord's delight to draw us close to Himself so that He may give us the healing and restoration that David spoke of.[7] In the well-known Bible passage, *John 15:1-17* (a real under-liner passage in your Bible, if there ever was one!), Jesus tells us it is the Father's pleasure – *His glory* – that we bear much fruit.[8] It is His heart's desire that we each have significant, fruitful, and fulfilling lives while we live and breathe here on planet Earth. However, why is it we so often get hung up on our hang-ups like I experienced for much of my life?

Does anyone remember the old-fashioned record albums? It was how we Boomers used to listen to music. You under-thirty folks may need to look this up on Wikipedia. When a record player needle was stuck in a scratch on the vinyl album, it would repeat the same section of words over, and over, and over again. Totally annoying!

Well, we humans are like that: scratched, wounded, and broken.

Often we find ourselves unable to get past habits and behaviors we despise or thought patterns we can't seem to break in our own strength. Like a scratched record album of long ago, we keep repeating the same issues over, and over, and over again. When Jesus said we would know the truth and the truth would set us free,[9] we know this to be, well...the truth! Yet, how do we get there?

Let's go back to the beginning.

Created in His Image...

We are created in the image of God.[10] We truly are fearfully and wonderfully made![11] There isn't one among us who can say otherwise, though we may be tempted to question that statement at times.

Although our pea-sized brains can't grasp the magnitude of the Trinity – God the Father, God the Son, and God the Holy Spirit, each co-equal, co-divine, co-existent, and co-eternal – the Bible maintains this truth over and over again. We too, are tri-part beings: *body*, *soul*, and *spirit*.

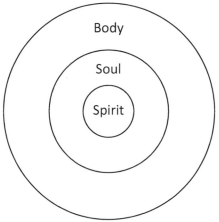

This simple diagram helps us understand the apostle Paul's words describing how God created us:

> *"Now may the God of peace Himself sanctify you
> completely; and may your whole **spirit**, **soul**, and **body**
> be preserved blameless at the coming of our Lord
> Jesus Christ."*
> 1 Thessalonians 5:23

Yes, we "get" that we have a body. There is not too much we don't understand about that fact. Our body lets us know all too well of its functions and dysfunctions; its pleasures and its pains. Anyone who has ever attended a Weight Watchers meeting has firsthand testimony of the power of our physical being! Our bodies are where our physical senses are located: taste, touch, sight, hearing, and smell. However, we also have a *soul* and a *spirit*. A better understanding of these unseen parts of our lives – what Paul calls the "inner man"[12] – will aid us in cooperating with the Lord's *refreshing*, *restoration*, and *renewal* in our lives, especially in the area of our thoughts.

Who We Are...

Let's first visit the deepest part of who we are: our *spirit*.

The same New Testament Greek word is used both for our *spirit* and for the Holy *Spirit*.

Pneuma Greek: Compare with the English "pneumonia," "pneumatology." Meaning breath, breeze, current of air, wind, and spirit.

Wow! What a perfect description of the Holy Spirit! Just as we can't actually see the wind swirling around us, we can certainly see the effects of it on everything it touches. We see trees move, we feel its touch on our cheeks, we see it dislodge the smallest feather or topple gigantic trees depending on its force. Just as the wind may be a gentle whisper of a breeze or a hurling-twirling mass of air current known as a tornado or hurricane, so it is with the Spirit of the living God. Though we can't physically *see* the Holy Spirit, we can feel, sense, and see the effects of His presence at work in our lives and in those around us.[13]

Our spirit cannot be seen either, but we certainly can sense and experience its presence when indwelt by the Holy Spirit.

> *"But as it is written: "Eye has not seen, nor ear heard, Nor have entered into the heart of man The things which God has prepared for those who love Him.*
> *But God has revealed them to us through His Spirit. For the Spirit searches all things, yes, the deep things of God.*
> *For what man knows the things of a man except the spirit of the man which is in him? Even so no one knows the things of God except the Spirit of God.*
> *Now we have received, not the spirit of the world, but the Spirit who is from God, that we might know the things that have been freely given to us by God."*
> 1 Corinthians 2:9-12

For us to know and experience all that God has freely given to us, our spirits must first be *born again*. Born of the Holy Spirit.

Born Again...

Do you recall in the Gospel of John when Nicodemus, a ruler of the Jews, came to Jesus at night to inquire more about Him? When answering his questions, Jesus told him he must be *born again* to see the kingdom of heaven.[14] Jesus specifically told Nic that what is born of the flesh is flesh, and that which is born of the Holy Spirit is spirit.[15] To understand what it means to be born again, we need to step back into the first book of the Bible.

In the Garden of Eden we see that God formed Adam. He then *breathed* into Adam's nostrils the *breath of life* and Adam became a living being.[16] This very *breath* of God is the *Holy Spirit* that gave life to Adam's *spirit*. What a tender moment of God imparting *His* life into the man of dust.

However, Adam and his partner in crime, Eve, blew it in a huge way (to say the least!). When they disobeyed God in the Garden, the eternal part of them, their God-breathed spirit *died*. They were cut off from the sweet communion they previously had with God. In their rebellious state they could no longer stand in the presence of God and survive the purity of His holiness, just as the Lord had forewarned them.[17] A great chasm opened up between God and sinful man as spiritual and physical death (along with all of hell's evil intent) were introduced into the once beautifully breathtaking and innocent world.

Adam's act of disobedience had great ramifications. Paul explains to us in the New Testament that Adam's spiritual death was passed onto us:

> *"Therefore, just as through one man sin entered the world, and death through sin, and thus death spread to all men, because all sinned..."*
> Romans 5:12

Like Adam, after his fall from God's perfect design, our *spirit,* is without life. Quite bluntly, the eternal part of us that God had originally created to commune with us and we with Him, is dead. Because Adam's sin and spiritual death infected us as well, coupled with our own sin (our literal *missing the mark* of God's holiness, purity, and perfection), we have been eternally separated from God. We need the Holy Spirit, Who is fully God, to bring us spiritually to life again. We must be *born again of the Spirit*. We need His *life-breath* to breathe into and revive our lifeless spirits.

How can this take place? In our sinful, spiritually dead condition, we are unable to save ourselves. Who will take the death penalty for us that we might live? Who will rescue us from ourselves and our sin?

Only the sinless, perfect sacrifice of Jesus – completely God, born in the flesh – could once and for all[18] restore fallen man to the eternal embrace of the Father. In Jesus' death, He bore the death penalty for our sin. When we by *faith, and faith alone*, receive this free gift of Jesus' sacrifice on the cross *in our place*, the Holy Spirit breathes His life into our spirit, taking up residence there. We are *born again* of the Holy Spirit and have renewed right standing and communion with God as His child.[19] This choice of ours to *believe* causes our *spirit* that was dead in sin to become *alive*.[20] The Spirit's life-breath overcoming our spiritual death as sons of Adam – heavenly CPR![21]

> "*For as many as are led by the Spirit of God, these are sons of God.*
>
> *For you did not receive the spirit of bondage again to fear, but you received the Spirit of adoption by whom we cry out, "Abba, Father."*
>
> *The Spirit Himself bears witness with our spirit that we are children of God,"*
> Romans 8:14-16

The Holy Spirit within us is a pledge or guarantee of all that is our inheritance as God's children.[22] Our made alive, born again *spirit* can now enjoy communion with the Most Holy God.[23] Because the Holy Spirit now dwells within us, we have access to His wonder-filled gifts that display His love and power.[24] As we learn to walk in the Spirit, His exquisite and delightful fruit – love, joy, peace, and patience...are naturally borne out in our lives because He is indwelling the deepest part of us.[25]

Introducing Our Soul...

Yet, so much of the time we are overwhelmed by our old "flesh nature" and we seem incapable of truly living in the Spirit. We often find our thoughts and lives in a tug-of-war match between what we know the Lord wants us to do and the behaviors, habits, and desires that want to take us in a completely opposite direction. That is where I found myself for so many years. Paul had this same struggle, too (at least I'm in good company!):

> *"For what I am doing, I do not understand. For what I will to do, that I do not practice; but what I hate, that I do."*
> Romans 7:15

I don't know about you, but it seemed like Paul's sentiment described my life most of the time. I knew the Holy Spirit lived inside of me, I just couldn't understand, however, why it was so hard to live in the abundant life Jesus had promised. My thoughts and actions were at constant odds with what I knew to be the truth.

Our Lord Jesus and the writers of the New Testament consistently remind us that our choice to live carnally, or in the flesh, can quench and undermine the work of the Holy Spirit in our lives. That doesn't mean the Spirit has left us, but that there is another segment of our lives that needs a little, no...rather, a *lot* of work! It is this area of our *soul* that causes us so much trouble.

It will be helpful to look at the Greek definition for the translation of the word *soul* found in our Bibles:

Psyche Greek: Compare with the English "psychology," "psychiatry," "psyche." To breathe, blow, life, person. The immaterial part of a man's being with the features of self-consciousness, will, reason, and conscience. Specifically, the **soul** is the seat of a person's emotions, thoughts, ability to choose, will, desires, affections, passions, and intellect. Simply, the **soul** is the place of the ***heart and mind*** of a person and what we would term their *personality*. The *soul* is that which strictly belongs to the person himself.

The definition we just read explains a lot. The soul is where our unruly *minds* and our broken and wounded *hearts* reside. When we were born again, our spirits experienced rebirth and were filled with the Holy Spirit. Our souls however – our hearts and minds – are still susceptible to our own sinful nature and failings, our enemy the devil, and the influences that come from the world we live in.

Whew! A triple-whammy! Because of our sinful nature, the enemy, and the world, we are engaged in a life-long process of our souls (and bodies as we will soon learn) being brought into submission to the Holy Spirit. The Bible terms this *sanctification* – the working of the Spirit to transform us into the image of Jesus.

Oh how I have wished that this could take place with a snap of my fingers! Don't you? I long for the total healing and transformation of my heart's emotions, the thoughts of my mind, and my physical actions to become a life that brings Him glory. I have often questioned the Lord as to why this process takes so long. Yet this is what a personal relationship with Jesus is all about; our absolute daily dependence upon His love and power as He transforms us from glory to glory.[26]

Our Hearts...

Think of it! Our *soul* is where our *heart* is located. Often in the Bible, these two words – *soul* and *heart* – are used interchangeably. Our *soul* is the seat of the broad spectrum of emotions that we experience: love and hurt, passion and apathy, joy and sorrow.

Here is the Greek New Testament definition for the English word translated *heart* in our Bibles:

Kardia Greek- meaning: Compare with "cardiac," or "cardiology." The physical organ of the body, the center of physical life, the seat of one's personal life (both physical and spiritual), the center of one's personality, the seat of one's entire mental and moral activity, containing both rational and emotional elements. It is the place of one's feelings, desires, joy, pain, and love.

> *"I will give you a **new heart** and put a **new spirit** in you; I will remove from you your **heart of stone** and give you a **heart of flesh**.*
> *And I will put my Spirit in you and move you to follow my decrees and be careful to keep my laws."*
> Ezekiel 26:26-27 NIV

These words take on new meaning as we realize the vastness of our *heart* and our need for Jesus' healing touch. His powerful Holy Spirit is the agent of transformation in our lives. This same Spirit that raised Jesus from the dead is now at work in our *heart* to raise them up, as well.[27]

He wants to replace our stony, messed-up heart with His heart...There could be no sweeter exchange.

More Regarding the Soul...

Our *soul* is also where our reasoning, intellect, and choice-making capabilities reside. In other words, our *soul* is where our *mind* and *our thought life takes place.*

Dianoia Greek – meaning: Mind. Literally, "a thinking through." The word suggests understanding, insight, meditation, reflection, perception, the gift of apprehension, the faculty of thought.

> *"And you shall love the LORD your God with all your*
> *heart, with all your soul, with all your **mind**, and with*
> *all your strength.' This is the first commandment."*
> Mark 12:30

Here, Jesus tells us to engage our whole soul and body (strength) in our love for Him. Yet He reminds us that we can't do anything without His help. Intimately knowing Him and His Word are key to walking in the Spirit.[28]

I must interject an important note at this time: Often when reading God's Word we will see the words *soul, heart, mind,* and *spirit,* used interchangeably (especially in the Old Testament). Both our *soul* (our heart and mind) and *spirit* are immaterial and unseen. They are uniquely linked together, the eternal part of us.

Often what we sense in our *spirit* affects our emotions and thoughts, such as when Paul tells us the Holy Spirit will bear witness with our spirit. Peter talks about women having a "gentle and quiet spirit" in a way that speaks of a gentle and quiet nature or personality.[29] This side of heaven, we won't understand completely how beautifully the Lord has wired us. However, as the author of Hebrews states, He by His word can cut to the dividing line of the *soul* and *spirit* and lay bare what is hidden deep inside of us.[30]

Our life choices strongly affect just about everything in our lives. *What* and *how* we *think* about our lives, and the world around us, colors everything we do. Our *thoughts* have a profound effect upon the *emotions* of our heart, and our *heart* has an amazing effect upon the way we *think*. We often cannot discern that our emotions and thoughts are not one and the same, most of the time. Indeed, there are many Bible passages that speak of the *thoughts* of the *heart*.[31] This is how tightly woven our mind and heart is. We now recognize when the Bible writers talk about the *soul*, they are also speaking of the vast arena of our *personality* and literally everything about us.

Yikes! The Flesh...

When the New Testament writers, predominantly Paul, write about *the flesh*, we can see the connection our *soul* has with the lusts and desires of our physical *body*. We know up-close and personal that *the* flesh gets us nowhere when it comes to being transformed into the image of Jesus, and He confirms this truth.[32] We can only be changed as the Holy Spirit moves in our lives, from the inside-out. Paul speaks to us through the ages when he chides the Galatian church:

> *"Are you so foolish? Having begun in the Spirit, are*
> *you now being made perfect by the flesh?"*
> Galatians 3:3

When we allow our *flesh* to call the shots in our lives, we limit or completely nullify the working of the Holy Spirit. Jesus said:

> *"It is the Spirit who gives life; the flesh profits*
> *nothing. The words that I speak to you are spirit, and*
> *they are life."*
> John 6:63

Paul writes:

> *"So then, those who are in the flesh cannot please God.*
> *But you are not in the flesh but in the Spirit, if indeed the Spirit of God dwells in you. Now if anyone does not have the Spirit of Christ, he is not His."*
> Romans 8:8-9

The scenarios that might demonstrate the interworking of our thoughts, heart and physical body (the flesh) are infinite in number…and that is just in the span of one hour of our lives!

Think About It…

Let's say you are experiencing a rather "blue" day. It is due to your best friend having lunch with another person whom you don't really care for. This has triggered feelings (emotions) of sadness due to insecurities arising from events that took place in your family years ago, though you may not realize that is the root of your issue. Your mind is soon filled with negative thoughts about yourself that devalue your worth.

From these spiraling downward feelings of sadness, your thoughts turn to despair of being abandoned and old fears of being alone soon follow. To comfort yourself you indulge in behaviors that bring solace for a moment: overeating, inappropriate images on your tablet or simply going back to bed and pulling the covers over your head. A few hours later you feel tremendous guilt for what you have done and ask the Lord's forgiveness for the eleven-hundredth time. The guilt lasts for three days, rendering you virtually powerless to be the person God has called you to be and to experience all that He has for you.

Maybe you have had a fairly nice day. However, when you arrive home from work your wife greets you at the door with the news that your son has once again ditched school and gone to a friend's home to play video games. Immediately, you fly into a fit of rage from the somewhat happy and pleasant mood you have been in all day. Without thinking, you pick up the nearest object and hurl it against the wall. "Where is he?" you yell as you march in anger toward your son's door, all the while pushing back your wife who is trying to prevent World War III. Minutes later you find yourself filled with remorse for the things you have said and done, and for the damage you have inflicted on a young man who is struggling to find his way.

These scenarios, some mild and some devastating, play out in our lives *each* and *every day*. The workings of our *flesh*, that is our *soul* (mind and heart), along with the urges and reactions of our *physical being* are the source of much of our heartbreak and suffering. Both to ourselves and to others. We ache to become more Christ-like, yet the ability to do so seems impossible. So what we are now learning – though it may seem tedious – has great bearing on our lives as Christians.

It is at this wearying point in our lives, the exceedingly great news of the gospel comes to our rescue.

Let's Walk in the Spirit...

> *"I say then: Walk in the Spirit, and you shall not fulfill the lust of the flesh."*
> Galatians 5:16

It's time to come under the influence of the Holy Spirit![33]

> *"O wretched man that I am! Who will deliver me*

from this body of death?

I thank God--through Jesus Christ our Lord! So then, with the mind I myself serve the law of God, but with the flesh the law of sin."

"There is therefore now no condemnation to those who are in Christ Jesus, who do not walk according to the flesh, but according to the Spirit.
For the law of the Spirit of life in Christ Jesus has made me free from the law of sin and death."
Romans 7:24-25, 8:1-2

Yippee! Yes! Hallelujah! Glory! In the previous verses Paul tells us that, *yes*, our flesh desires and gravitates toward the old law (or nature) of sin that was at work in us. Nevertheless, he triumphantly states that the Holy Spirit of life in Jesus has released us from the bondage of that old law, and we no longer have to live like we once did. Yes, in Christ Jesus it *is* possible to experience *refreshing*, *restoration*, and *renewal*! Now we realize the significance King David's words in Psalm 23:3 at the opening of this chapter...

"...He refreshes (restores) my soul."

We will be reminded shortly that one way Paul invites us to be transformed is by the *renewing of our minds*.[34] What we allow into our thoughts plays a huge part in either hindering our journey in Jesus or propelling us to move forward, step by step. Will we fall sometimes? Yes of course. However, Jesus' immense treasury of limitless grace will pick us up from our skinned knees and strengthen us to press forward *in Him*.[35] As we allow the Holy Spirit to work in us, we are enabled to bring every thought captive to Christ.[36] We will find this opens the door for the unconditional love of our lavish Lord to heal our *hearts*. In Him we will find grace and peace beyond measure, fruitfulness beyond our wildest dreams, and fulfillment and satisfaction as we dance in the ocean of His refreshing presence.

Are you ready to press forward?

"Not that I have already attained, or am already perfected; but I press on, that I may lay hold of that for which Christ Jesus has also laid hold of me."
Philippians 3:12

Study Questions...

- How does knowing that Jesus wants to give you an abundant life encourage and challenge you?

- Why do you think that understanding the difference between your soul and spirit is helpful in discovering true transformation?

- Can you give a scenario from your own life where your mind, heart, and body seem to fall into old behavior patterns you can't seem to break free from? (Share only if comfortable in a group setting.)

- What does is mean for you to have the Good Shepherd restore your soul?

- Does walking in the Spirit consistently seem a little more possible for you since reading this chapter? Explain.

---

[1] John 10:11

[2] 2 Peter 1:4

[3] John 10:10

[4] Jeremiah 17:7-8

[5] Hebrews 13:5

[6] Matthew 5:14

[7] Luke 4:17-21

[8] John 15:8

[9] John 8:32

[10] Genesis 1:26

[11] Psalm 139:14

[12] Ephesians 3:16

[13] There are an infinite number of books and studies written about the third person of the Trinity, the Holy Spirit. . I suggest "Pneuma Life that can be found on Amazon.com or by contacting me at susanboldt@gmail.com. However, nothing can beat the reading of the New Testament to learn more about Him!

[14] John 3:1-8

[15] John 3:6

[16] Genesis 2:7

[17] 1 Corinthians 21-22

[18] Hebrews 7:27

[19] John 1:12

[20] Ephesians 2:5

[21] Romans 8:11

[22] Ephesians 1:13-14, 2 Corinthians 1:22

[23] John 15:9

[24] 1 Corinthians 12:7-10

[25] Galatians 5:22-23

[26] 2 Corinthians 3:18

[27] Ephesians 2:18-20

[28] John 15:1-17

[29] 1 Peter 4:6

[30] Hebrews 4:12

[31] Job 17:11, Daniel 2:30, Matthew 15:19

[32] John 6:63

[33] Ephesians 5:17-18

[34] Romans 12:2

[35] Ephesians 2:7

[36] 2 Corinthians 10:5

Times of Refreshing

*"Repent therefore and be converted, that your sins may be blotted out, so **that times of refreshing** may come **from the presence of the Lord,"***
Acts 3:19

Awwww…big sigh…

Who doesn't want to be refreshed? Add to that, to have refreshment from the *presence of the living God* – the Lord of light, life, hope, happiness, sweetness, power, and healing. Sounds pretty good to me!

"Therefore my heart is glad, and my whole being rejoices; my flesh also dwells secure.
…You make known to me the path of life; in your presence there is fullness of joy; at your right hand are pleasures forevermore."
Psalm 16:9, 11 ESV

What would it be like for my whole being – spirit, soul, and body – to rejoice? To know fullness of joy and peace? To rest securely and have a continual sense of God's presence, regardless of my circumstances?[1] Earlier in this psalm of David,[2] he writes that this is his inheritance –

our inheritance!

Repentance is Key...

I am reminded of the old but powerfully worded Christmas carol, "O, Holy Night." This beautiful song heralds the truth that Jesus' birth brings a "thrill of hope" to a person and that the "weary world" will rejoice.[3] However, you only have to watch the evening news or read the latest world happenings on your smart phone to know there is a disconnect somewhere. The truth of the matter is: our world is not the only thing that is joyless or weary. Sometimes we Christians are too.

Let's read again the opening Scripture verse for this chapter:

> *"Repent therefore and be converted, that your sins*
> *may be blotted out, so that times of refreshing may*
> *come from the presence of the Lord,"*
> Acts 3:19

Peter, preaching to the crowd that had assembled after the lame man was healed at Solomon's Portico, gives us the clearest instruction for how to find refreshment for our daily lives. The first step is: ***repentance.***

Arghhhhhh...any word but that word! *Repentance*! Oh my. I don't know about you, but I envision a hairy man, wearing hairy clothes, eating bugs, and standing in a river shouting out to me: "REPENT!!!" Not that I don't have a deep fondness for John the Baptist and his message that inspired the Hawaiian HE>i tee-shirt company,[4] but he scares me a little bit!

The word *repentance* just makes me feel...bad. I seem to fail at even attempting it. I have *tried* desperately to change areas of my life that cause me to live *less than* what Jesus has for me, but I often experience little to no success. I have said, *"I am sorry,"* a zillion times over for the same life issues to no avail, except to reap greater guilt. I feel badly about feeling badly all the time. Does anyone identify with me?

Possibly, have I missed or forgotten what *repentance* is really about? It can't only be about feeling sorry and horrible over behaviors that I can't seem to break free from. As genuine as my remorse has been, staying in the pit of remorse has brought me no closer to the freedom I know the Lord wants for me. His Word tells me that I am forgiven, but my mind tells me otherwise. No, if the Lord Jesus gave His disciples instruction to preach *repentance* as part of the *Good News* of the gospel[5] – just as Peter was doing in our opening passage – well, *repentance* must be…*good news*.

What is True Repentance?

The New Testament Greek word that is translated *repentance* in our English Bibles gives us insight.

Metanoeo Greek – Meaning: From *Meta* a change of place or condition; and *Noeo* to exercise the mind, think, comprehend. To think and comprehend differently. To undergo a moral change of direction because the mind has undergone a change. Though repentance can be expressed through sorrow (emotions), *it is more tied to the mind* (a choice) rather than to mere emotion.

Repentance is not just feeling remorse for our *missing the mark* of God's holiness (wholeness) and righteousness (rightness). Yes, Jesus tells us that our sorrow over our sin is a huge element in realizing the depths of His sacrifice and experiencing His love, however, sorrow alone is "not enough" to bring genuine transformation to our lives. Nor is *repentance* our trying harder to change our behaviors (though we will soon find out that genuine repentance *will* change our actions).

True repentance begins with a transformation in our *thoughts*. It is a paradigm shift in the way we think about and view life and, more urgently, how we think about and view our Almighty God who loves us beyond comprehension. It is also a change in viewing *what*, *how*, and *why* we do things that are displeasing to God, because they are harmful to *us*.

Instead of choosing to continue on the path of our self-centered thoughts or the world's way of thinking, repentance is the *surrender* and *exchange* of our thoughts for God's thoughts. Repentance causes us to experience a genuine renewal in our minds and consequently our hearts (remember how closely related these two are?).

Quite literally, repentance is a transformation in the *thoughts of our heart*. Repentance is the exchange of our trying to carry the burden and load of our lives and placing ourselves in the Lord's hands. Repentance is the surrender of our will for His will, recognizing we need the Savior desperately. In truth, repentance is a *U-turn*, from thinking and living in a certain direction and turning 180 degrees to go the Lord's way of thinking and living.

Peter reiterates this turning by punctuating the phrase "repent therefore and *be converted.*" To be *converted* in the original Greek language is to turn, be turned toward, and to embrace something. When this conversion or U-turn of repentance takes place in our hearts and minds, our actions will follow suit. Not the other way around.[6] To *repent* and be *converted* we must embrace God and **His** thoughts and ways.

Our First Step...

If you have chosen to believe and trust in the forgiving love of Jesus Christ as your Lord and receive Him by faith into your life,[7] that decision was your *first act of repentance*. Your heart was touched by the Holy Spirit as He revealed to you your great need for Him. Your acknowledgement of His Lordship in your thoughts, in response to the Spirit's tugging on your heartstrings, was a dramatic shift from how you had previously viewed your life, and probably your view of God. You may have only taken baby steps of repentance at that time, but baby steps count! For by His wondrous grace you have been saved.[8]

This decision to follow Jesus changes everything! This side of heaven, we will barely be able to grasp all that took place in that most magnificent moment. If we simply plunked ourselves in the letter Paul wrote to the Ephesian church, we could dwell there and meditate on these short chapters for the rest of our lives and still only scratch the surface of our God-given inheritance in Christ.

However, let's look at just a few of the marvelous things that took place in regard to our first act of repentance – when we asked the Lord Jesus to come into our heart – as we simply focus on Peter's brief words in Acts 3:19. Let's read this verse again:

> *"Repent therefore and be converted, that your **sins may be blotted out**, so **that times of refreshing** may come **from the presence of the Lord**,"*

Numero uno, our sins were *blotted out* at the point of our faith for salvation. When I think of *blotting* something out, it sounds a bit tame to me – much like trying to remove a stain from a tablecloth by dabbing at it gently. However, the New King James Version for the phrase, *"blotted out,"* in regard to God's forgiveness of our sin, actually means *wiped out, erased, eradicated,* and *obliterated* in the original Greek language of the New Testament. This certainly is much stronger wording to describe the Lord's gift of pardon to us!

Instead of the Father seeing every wrong act, word, deed, thought or motive we have that would keep us from an intimate relationship with Him, He now sees the sacrificial death and resurrection of His Son wiping our slates clean.[9] This is our one and only basis for right-standing with God. We cannot add to this marvelous and scandalous grace He has extended to us; nor can we subtract from it. It is the free, unmerited gift of God for His children.

Because the shed blood of Jesus Christ has erased and obliterated our sin which kept us from communion and fellowship with God, we now have full access to His very presence.

> *"Therefore, brethren, having boldness to enter the Holiest by the blood of Jesus,*
> *by a new and living way which He consecrated for us, through the veil, that is, His flesh,*
> *and having a High Priest over the house of God,*
> *let us draw near with a true heart in full assurance of faith, having our hearts sprinkled from an evil conscience and our bodies washed with pure water.*
> *Let us hold fast the confession of our hope without wavering, for He who promised is faithful."*
> Hebrews 10:19-23

Jesus invites His children into a personal and intimate daily relationship with Him. We can draw near to Him with full assurance of faith and in His presence is **everything we need**: peace, joy, provision, strength, healing, and comfort; no matter what our current circumstances are. The list of His gifts towards us is limitless because He is limitless. We cannot help but be refreshed by His lavish presence in our daily lives.

The River...

"On the last day, that great day of the feast, Jesus stood and cried out, saying, "If anyone thirsts, let him come to Me and drink.

"He who believes in Me, as the Scripture has said, out of his heart will flow rivers of living water."

But this He spoke concerning the Spirit, whom those believing in Him would receive; for the Holy Spirit was not yet given, because Jesus was not yet glorified."
John 7:37-39

The *times of refreshing* Peter spoke about come directly from the words of the Master he loved so much. It is the **Holy Spirit** indwelling our spirit that overflows into every area of our lives. He brings *refreshing*, *restoration*, and *renewal* – much like a powerful, surging river full of *living* water.

The Holy Spirit comes to dwell in every person who believes in Jesus Christ for salvation. The Spirit (the third Person of the God-head) reveals Jesus to us. He convinces us of God's rightness, transforms our lives to bear the image of Christ, and empowers us with His gifts for spiritual battle against our enemy. He is the One who comes along side of us and is our great Comforter and Counselor. Oh my! What a "nutshell" version of the Spirit's tremendous work in the life of a Christian!

"For you did not receive the spirit of bondage again to fear, but you received the Spirit of adoption by whom we cry out, "Abba, Father."

45

The Spirit Himself bears witness with our spirit that we
are children of God,"
Romans 8:15-16

It is the Holy Spirit who bears witness in *our* spirit that we are *truly* God's child. He is the seal or guarantee of our salvation. It is the spiritual overflow from the Holy Spirit residing in our spirit that causes unspeakable joy within us. We experience outrageous love and phenomenal peace in such profound measure, *regardless of what we are going through*. In fact, it is when our lives are most squeezed and pressured that His abundance in us is so evident to others – if we let Him be Lord. This is the life Christians were meant to have. Yet, after many years as a Christian, I found myself struggling to walk in the Spirit's provision for me.

Where was the excitement and transforming power I had known the first few years of walking with Jesus? Why couldn't I maintain the spiritual high of a retreat or conference beyond just a few weeks? Because I wasn't living a daily satisfied, overflowing, abundant life in my heart and mind, I began looking to the world to meet my longings and insecurities.

Looking for Fulfillment...

Do you remember reading Jesus' words in the last chapter speaking of abundant life? Well, I'd failed to place close attention on the first phrase of His words found in John 10:10a:

> *"**The** thief **does not come except to steal, and to kill, and to destroy**. I have come that they may have life, and that they may have it more abundantly."*

I had not guarded my mind and heart from the one who would

steal, kill, and destroy me; and it was in my mind and heart that my battle raged. I could not, for the life of me, seem to walk in the overcoming and exhilarating power of the Holy Spirit that once used to shower my life in my early Christian years. I was not experiencing the abundant, more-than-enough, profuse life that Jesus promises His followers.

As we read God's written Word, the Holy Spirit constantly speaks to us that the battle must first be won in our mind and heart – our *soul*. Please forgive me for saying this, but the majority of us, myself included, are so careless with our mind and heart. We want to put the cart-before-the horse and have our *actions* renewed: stay on that diet, stop yelling at the kids, have victory over retail therapy, be free of pornography, quit having hurt feelings all the time, stop abusing a substance – you name it. We want our areas of failure to stop without dealing with the source of our anguish; our thought and heart life. However, God puts a high premium on *what we think* and what we *allow* into the *emotions of our heart*. If we don't get this truth settled first, the transformation of our lives will be stalled as if in quicksand.

His Love Alone...

God has always known what we need. His Word is filled with story-after-story of His passionate pursuit of men and women to realize that His love is the *only* love we need. However, our adversary takes advantage of our faulty and broken human love and turns what was intended for such beauty into ashes in our hands. Our *hearts* and *minds* have been opened up to terrible damage from the thief who only comes to rob, kill, and destroy us, and to turn us away from God's love.

In the Old Testament (before Jesus walked on the earth), God used the nation of Israel as an example of the urgency of His love message for mankind. He told them:

> *"Take **heed** to yourselves, lest your **heart be deceived**, and you turn aside and serve other gods and worship them,*
> *"lest the LORD's anger be aroused against you, and He shut up the heavens so that there be no rain, and the land yield no produce, and you perish quickly from the good land which the LORD is giving you.*
>
> *"Therefore **you shall lay up these words of mine in your heart and in your soul**, and bind them as a sign on your hand, and they shall be as frontlets between your eyes."*
> Deuteronomy 11:16-18

We see here the intense instruction of the Lord for Israel to take *great caution* regarding their minds and hearts. Israel was not to think the way the rest of the world did. God did not want them (or us!) to be seduced by the god of this world[10] and thereby be robbed of the incredible fruitfulness that He had in store for them. God even uses the Old Testament version of "sticky notes" (frontlets or phylacteries) to remind them of His life-giving word. Thank the Holy Spirit for now residing in us New Testament believers to recall God's Word to our minds – I don't think I could carry out that Old Testament fashion statement!

Throughout the Old Testament the Lord beckons to us (through the nation Israel) to *repentance* of the mind and heart because He knows our actions will follow. Simply put, but so hard for us to grasp: the Lord Almighty wants a love relationship with us, His dear lambs.[11] He knows that He alone is the only One who can satiate our lives to overflowing.[12] He knows that the torrential flooding of His

48

love in our heart will transform our missing-the-mark, sinful ways into glorious lives from the inside out with His fullness, grace for grace.[13]

Abundance...

"Ho! Everyone who thirsts, Come to the waters; And you who have no money, Come, buy and eat. Yes, come, buy wine and milk Without money and without price.

*Why do you spend money for what is not bread, And your wages for what does not satisfy? Listen carefully to Me, and eat what is good, And let your **soul** delight itself in **abundance**.*

Incline your ear, and come to Me. Hear, and your soul shall live; And I will make an everlasting covenant with you--The sure mercies of David."
Isaiah 55:1-3

Doesn't that sound good? That our soul – our heart and mind – would be delighted in such abundance? Would the stuff that hangs us up so much even matter? I don't think so. And, He continues...

"Seek the LORD while He may be found, Call upon Him while He is near.

*Let the wicked forsake his way, And the unrighteous man his **thoughts**; Let him return to the LORD, And He will have mercy on him; And to our God, For He will abundantly pardon.*

*"For **My thoughts are not your thoughts**, Nor are your ways My ways," says the LORD.*

*"For as the heavens are higher than the earth, So are My ways higher than your ways, And **My thoughts** than your thoughts.*
Isaiah 55:6-9

This is the center of true repentance. This is what John the Baptist was crying out from the Jordan River. God's Word calls out to us to forsake *our* thoughts and *our* ways for the Lord's thoughts and ways. Let us draw near to God, and He will ever so tenderly and graciously draw near to us with His love and power.[14] As we exchange our filthy-ragged, less-than life for His robe-of-glorious-righteousness-life, we need to guard this new way of thinking as the most precious prize we own.

> *"Keep your heart with all diligence,*
> *For out of it spring the issues of life."*
> Proverbs 4:23

If you read the introduction to this book, you know I didn't do this. I did not give diligence to my heart by means of my thoughts. I did not guard my *soul,* and I paid dearly for this grave mistake.

John Eldredge in his book, "Waking the Dead," puts this in perspective:

> *"The heart (and subsequently the mind) is central. That we would even need to be reminded of this only shows how far we have fallen from the life we were meant to live – of how powerful the spell (of the enemy) has been. The subject of the heart is addressed in the Bible more than any other topic – more than works or service, more than belief or obedience, more than money, and even more than worship. Maybe God knows something we've forgotten. But of course – all those other things are matters of the heart."[15]*

Our hearts have always been "*what it's about*" when it comes to the Lord. The religious leaders of Jesus' day had righteousness down to a formula. They followed the Law of Moses and, if that wasn't enough, they instituted rules and regulations for anything and everything under the sun to-do or not-do. However, Jesus called them hypocrites and whitewashed graves where death resided inside. They had missed the point of God's law, which was righteousness (rightness) and holiness (wholeness) stemming from the place where life flows – the heart.

I had the same type of blindness as these religious leaders. Over the years I had drifted so far from the truth of His Word that I couldn't differentiate between a lie of the enemy, the world, or my own thoughts.[16] I knew the Word of God, but had grown cold in applying it to my life and genuinely believing it.

As I found myself entrenched in habits and behaviors that hindered my walk with the Lord, I repeatedly tried to change my failings, struggling to correct the outside, but I was not dealing with the core issues of my thought life and heart. I asked for prayer and sought counsel several times for these issues and I received genuine help at each juncture, however, I did not find the lasting freedom that I longed for.

One Saturday Morning...

Yet the Lord never gave up on me! Part of my struggle was possibly laziness in pursuing it. He wanted me to *want* freedom badly enough. I have also come to recognize that another aspect of my struggle was the work of the Holy Spirit. He was increasing my hunger to know the Lord with an intimacy that would not have taken place if He had just thrown pixie-dust on me and cleaned up my act with a spiritual magic wand.

"For I know the thoughts that I think toward you, says the LORD, thoughts of peace and not of evil, to give you

a future and a hope."
Jeremiah 29:11

Oh, how we all love and cherish this precious verse! However, I had not looked closely at the verses immediately following it:

> *"Then you will call upon Me and go and pray to Me, and I will listen to you.*
>
> *And you will **seek Me** and find Me, when **you search for Me** with **all your heart**.*
>
> *I will be found by you, says the LORD, and **I will bring you back from your captivity**; I will gather you from all the nations and from all the places where I have driven you, says the LORD, and I will bring you to the place from which I cause you to be carried away captive."*
> Jeremiah 29:12-14

The note referenced from the passage above in *The New Spirit Filled Life Bible* sheds further light on these verses:

> *"Throughout Scripture we find repeated references to God's people seeking after Him. Implied in these passages is a quest for God that includes a level of intensity beyond what might be termed ordinary prayer. The word "search' along with the phrase "with all your heart" suggests an earnestness that borders on desperation. The word "search" (Hebrew **darash**) suggests a "following after," or close pursuit of a desired objective; it also implies a diligence in the searching process. In 2 Chronicles 15:2, Azariah promises the Lord will be with His people if they "seek" (**darash**) after Him – another indicator of God's emphasis on intensity and diligence in prayer."[17]*

I will never underestimate His workings and what He might use to bring us into His embrace. He didn't just want me to be free: Jesus wanted me to **know** Him in such a way that would *rock* me and *rock* the world around me.

I have shared how, in the midst of the depression and the desperation I felt for all of my futile efforts, the Lord rescued me.[18] Not that He wasn't always there waiting for my heart to respond to His; however, I'm just not sure how much I really wanted to change from deep within – I had wanted the quick fix. He, however, wanted me to **want Him more** than my deliverance. He genuinely and completely broke my depression in an instant. One arrow from Jesus' heart to mine sent that bad boy of *pride* packing.

In exchange, the Lord asked me for a complete surrender of all my affections for the world – even my family and ministry – to declare that He was the only One I wanted to live for. This has been on on-going surrender which will take place in my life and your life *every* day *of our lives* as long as we have breath. It is not a one-time surrender, but a continual turning and embracing of God instead of doing or trying what I think is best. Big laugh. When has that ever been profitable or a good decision? I had first come to the Lord out of my need and what I could get from Him. He was now calling me to seek Him only for Himself, not for anything He could do for me.

This surrender was a radical difference in my journey as a Christian. It seemed as if I was jumping off a cliff into a great unknown abyss and truthfully this was a much harder decision on my part than my initial decision to follow Jesus! I was older and had more stuff to give up! In His great love, however, He was there to catch me and uphold me with His everlasting arms.[19]

Even when there are still days I might try to take back the reins of my life, the Lord never gives up on me as He is kneading my heart to desire only Him, cleansing my mind, and causing me to live differently than I ever have before.[20] This new-found surrender took time, and *it still takes time*! This side of heaven I will always be a work in progress, but what a difference it makes to walk in freedom and not just learn to cope with my issues.

Looking Back...

Soon after the breakthrough I experienced from depression, I remember very clearly asking Jesus *how* I had allowed this *mess* to happen that He was drawing me out of. He spoke ever so gently and tenderly to me:

> *"These people draw near to Me with their mouth, And honor Me with their lips, But their **heart** is far from Me."*
> Matthew 15:8

Ouch! My attempts to be a Christian were just as hypocritical as the religious Pharisees that Jesus was speaking to here. To show for it: my life revealed unhappiness, frustration, and discouragement. Up to this point I had not been able to understand why and how the enemy had captured me with such a death-grip of fantasy, an eating disorder, and depression while I was still doing all the Christian stuff that Christians are privileged to do. But in God's economy, most of my Bible reading, praying, going to church, and a million other things were not worth a hill of beans if my *heart* was far from Him. My *mind* was reading, viewing, and fantasying about things I should never have allowed.

I now realize that guarding my mind and heart is of utmost importance. What am I exposing my mind and heart to? I want to keep Jesus as Numero Uno in my affections and thoughts. By doing this, everything else will fall into place.[21] I didn't say life would be easy. Nevertheless, when the distractions of the enemy, the world, and my own brokenness bow to His Lordship, His kingdom will take preeminence in my earthy situations.[22] Glory! And, as I begin the practice of capturing every thought I have to the obedience of Christ, my life will be continually *refreshed*, *restored*, and *renewed*.[23]

> *"And you He made alive, who were dead in trespasses and sins,*
> *in which you once walked according to the course of this world, according to the prince of the power of the air, the spirit who now works in the sons of disobedience,*
> *among whom also we all once conducted ourselves in the **lusts of our flesh, fulfilling the desires of the flesh and of the mind**, and were by nature children of wrath, just as the others."*
> Ephesians 2:1-3

Gosh! No wonder I couldn't find the freedom I'd once known as a young believer. I had reverted back to walking *according to the course of this world*, letting my guard down and allowing the *prince of* the *power of the air* (the devil) to capture large chunks of my soul.

No wonder *Jesus* tells us to:

- Keep our hearts pure.[24]
- Be careful about what our hearts treasure and hold dear.[25]
- Carefully sow His word in our hearts.[26]
- Forgive others from our heart.[27]
- Love God with all of our heart, soul, mind, and strength.[28]
- Not harden our hearts.[29]
- Cultivate God's goodness in our hearts.[30]
- Guard our hearts and our thoughts because the words of our mouth (and how we live) will be affected.[31]

- Not lose heart and become discouraged.[32]
- Not be troubled in our hearts, but believing Him.[33]
- Not be anxious or worried in our hearts.[34]

No wonder **Paul** tells us to:

- Set our minds (and affections in some Bible translations) on things above and not on earthly ways of thinking![35]
- Put on the *breastplate* of righteousness or God's rightness (guarding our hearts) and the *helmet* of salvation (protecting our minds).[36]
- Be renewed by the transformation of our minds.[37]
- Walk in the mind of Christ.[38]
- Bring every thought captive to the obedience of Christ.[39]
- Be spiritually minded, not worldly minded because the peace of our hearts and our very lives are on the line.[40]
- Be anxious for nothing, but surrender our cares to Him so that His peace will guard our hearts and minds.[41]
- Have our thoughts dwell only on those things that are true, noble, pure, and lovely.[42]
- Not walk in fear, but live in the self-control and power of a sound mind.[43]

No wonder **Peter** tells us to:

- Gird up the loins of our minds so that we won't return to former failings and deceptions![44]
- Be careful in the activities that we engage in that can become a struggle or war for our souls.[45]
- Be thoughtful and diligent about how we walk in this broken world because we have an adversary seeking for the tiniest opportunity to take advantage of us.[46]
- Be observant so that we are not deceived.[47]

*"For where your treasure is, there your **heart** will be also."*
Luke 12:34

Moving Forward...

If there is any help to be found in this book, it is only because the Spirit of God has brought you to a place that only He can only bring you to. He alone can speak words to you that will be transforming and freeing to your soul. The Lord will not use a cookie-cutter formula, though the principles of His Word will be the same anchors of truth that have set countless of His loved ones free through the ages. He will speak to you individually as you seek Him ardently.[48] *Repentance* won't be a scary word but a gateway to life-giving *times of refreshing* in His presence that can bring clarity to your thoughts and wholeness to your heart.

Now, we are moving forward!

"Now hope does not disappoint, because the love of God has been poured out in our hearts by the Holy Spirit who was given to us."
Romans 5:5

Study Questions...

- Rewrite the phrase *"repent and be converted"* from Peter's discourse into your own words.

- Describe what it means to have the Holy Spirit living inside of you as *a river of living water*.

- Can you identify with desiring transformation in areas of your life, but wanting a quick fix? Elaborate.

- Has your heart ever drifted from first love with the Lord *Revelation 2:4*. What was the outcome?

- Review Jesus', Paul's, and Peter's words of encouragement on pages 55 and 56. Which do you find the hardest to pursue, and why?

[1] Jeremiah 17:7-8

[2] Psalm 16:6

[3] "O Holy Night," Adolphe Adam, 1847; John Sullivan Dwight 1855.

[4] http://hegreaterthani.com

[5] Luke 24:47

[6] Matthew 12:35

[7] John 1:12

[8] Ephesians 2:8-9

[9] 1 Corinthians 1:30

[10] 1 John 5:19

[11] Isaiah 40:11

[12] Jeremiah 31:14

[13] John 1:16

[14] James 4:8

[15] John Eldredge, Waking the Dead, (Nashville, TN: Thomas Nelson, Inc., 2003), page 39. (Words in italics are mine – given for clarity.)

[16] Romans 12:2

[17] Jack W. Hayford, Sr. Editor, New Spirit Filled Life Bible, (Nashville, TN: Thomas Nelson, Inc., 2002) Jeremiah 29:11-14, Dick Eastman, contributor

[18] Jeremiah 29:13-14

[19] Deuteronomy 33:27

[20] 2 Timothy 2:13

[21] Matthew 6:33

[22] Luke 11:2

[23] 2 Corinthians 2:3-5

[24] Matthew 5:8

[25] Matthew 6:21, Matthew 12:35

[26] Matthew 13:19

[27] Matthew 18:35

[28] Mark 12:30

[29] Mark 8:17

[30] Luke 6:45

[31] Mark 7:21

[32] Luke 18:1

[33] John 14:1

[34] Luke 12:29

[35] Colossians 3:1-3

[36] Ephesians 6:14

[37] Romans 12:2

[38] 1 Corinthians 2:16

[39] 2 Corinthians 10:5

[40] Romans 8:6

[41] Philippians 4:6-7

[42] Philippians 4:8

[43] 2nd Timothy 1:7

[44] 1 Peter 1:13-14

[45] 1 Peter 2:11

[46] 1 Peter 5:8

[47] 2 Peter 2:1

[48] Hebrews 11:6

Sweet Surrender

"I beseech you therefore, brethren, by the mercies of God, that you present your bodies a living sacrifice, holy, acceptable to God, which is your reasonable service.
Romans 12:1

It probably goes without saying…

If we truly want to be transformed into the image of our Beloved Savior, especially in the area of our thought lives, we need to surrender every aspect of ourselves to His Lordship. This means continual surrender, with our mind's choice, not just a one-time event in the height of an emotional moment.

Yikes! That's a doozy! Who thought that one up? You mean everything? Yes, everything.

*"So he answered and said, 'You shall love the LORD your God with all your **heart**, with all your **soul**, with all your **strength**, and with all your **mind**,' and 'your neighbor as yourself.' "*
Luke 10:27

This is just what we have been learning about! Loving God with all of our soul – encompassing our heart and mind – and with all of our strength – our body. It's not rocket science or jumping through spiritual hoops. He just wants us to fall in love with Him with all of our being. This is a paradigm shift from the way most of the world thinks about God and what our flesh would naturally choose (at first!).[1]

I have come to a place in my life where I want to experience and know God with all that is within me.[2] I long to be used to bring the healing power of His gospel to this broken and hurting world. Yet I still like to hold some areas of my life in reserve, especially my future. Still He is calling all of us to abandon our plans, dreams, desires, habits, actions, words, thoughts, and affections; yes, every ounce of our lives to Him.[3] I've heard our fear of relinquishment to God compared to our holding onto a stale moldy, half-eaten peanut butter and jelly sandwich, instead of sitting down to the feast He is presenting us: an endless-course meal filled with satisfying and filling delicacies, delights, and savories beyond belief.

Several years ago I sensed the still small voice of the Lord saying to me, "Sue, everything about Me is *free*; you can't earn or work your way into my great favor, you already have my absolute devotion and love just because I created you as my child. Though everything about Me is free, however, I am not *cheap*. To really know Me will cost you everything. I want all of you because I love you so very much. I can't give you everything I want to as long as your heart is still holding tightly onto so much that is not from Me."

My dear friend, Jaime Betters, told me recently that the Holy Spirit put the same question to her a few years ago, but with different wording: "Jaime, I can't plant all of my Word, my promises, and my love into the soil of your life and have them bloom abundantly while there are still so many weeds you are hanging onto. Please give your weeds to me and see what I plant in their place!"[4]

Jesus is always calling us to greater surrender and abandonment to Him. Offering ourselves as a *daily* sacrifice to the Lord will be our lifelong highest priority; though as someone once quipped, "The trouble with a living sacrifice is that it keeps crawling off the altar!"

However... Oh my! We can't even *do* surrender ourselves! God knows we are all broken and messed-up basket cases, as my wonderful friend, Debbie Alsdorf, likes to say. However, He still loves us with the greatest compassion and mercy.[5] He surrounds us, above and below, front and back – even when our hearts are furthest from Him.[6] He knows that our complete abandonment to Him is difficult.[7]

Even when we think we can't possibly give Him an area of our lives that He is targeting, if we ask the Holy Spirit to help us even *want* to place this area into Jesus' hands, the great Comforter will come to our rescue time after time.[8] I cannot recall how many times I've asked the Lord to make me willing *to be made willing.*

> *"I say then: Walk in the Spirit, and you shall not*
> *fulfill the lust of the flesh."*
> Galatians 5:16

I've come to think that this powerful verse simply states that as we come to the Lord daily, intentionally laying down our own agenda for that day to the work of the Holy Spirit, He will begin to take over. This is daily *surrender* and *repentance*. It will take a huge step of faith on our parts, but this is where the excitement of a daily walk with Jesus begins, no matter how mundane you think your life *now* is. Remember? This is Jesus, who turns water into wine.

Because He loves us so darn much, we can trust Him with

everything. That is the *reasonable* thing for us to do as Romans 12:1 tells us at the outset of this chapter. Our agendas are always skewed by our own selfishness, blindness, and faithlessness; His agenda is only motivated by pure, beyond-reason love for us. Why do we think *we* would know better about our lives than He? That was the same underlying lie that the serpent tempted Adam and Eve with in the Garden. I recently heard a great phrase, "If you want to give God a good laugh, tell Him your plans!"

Your Turn...

This might be a good place to stop and have a good *pouring out* time with the Lord before we proceed further.[9]   Has Jesus been sweetly and gently nudging you about an area of your life to abandon to Him? Even if nothing immediately comes to your mind, take a moment to ask the Holy Spirit to search your heart and reveal to you if there is any area of your life that you are holding onto. Please take time to do this, and do not rush through this moment. If you need the Spirit's help in placing something fully into the Lord's hands, ask Him to help you.

Don't worry if it takes a you few days...or weeks to let go of areas of your life that you have been holding onto. Surrender along with repentance, like many aspects of the Christian walk, can often take place in *layers*, little by little, but we have to start somewhere. Sometimes we have held a long, tight grip on "stuff." Take all of the time you need until you sense that you have truly released this/these area(s) in absolute surrender to the Lord.

The beloved verses below take on new meaning when we realize they are really an invitation for us to experience the sweetness and relief of full surrender to Jesus.

"casting all your care upon Him, for He cares for you."
1 Peter 5:7

"Come to Me, all you who labor and are heavy laden, and I will give you rest.
"Take My yoke upon you and learn from Me, for I am gentle and lowly in heart, and you will find rest for your souls.
"For My yoke is easy and My burden is light."
Matthew 11:28-30

Release often feels like a weight has been lifted from you; or you may experience a fresh sense of joy. A quiet calm may come over you or the contentment of peace. You may not experience anything, yet you can be assured that He took your burden even before you drew breath to pray and give it to Him. Only He is able to carry these cares that have become more like weeds in your life, rather than plantings of righteousness.

Should a sense of heaviness or worry come upon you, it is time to come back to a place of surrender…again. Don't delay! Don't let the devil bandy you about in your thoughts. Come quickly to the Lord Jesus. Linger in prayer and in the encouragement of God's Word until peace returns to you. If you are new to the Bible, turn to the middle of the Book, the Psalms. These are songs written by those who were surrendering their burdens, too. Make no mistake about it. God has our stuff in His hands, but sometimes it takes us a while to really let go of it!

Taking Next Steps...

Let's continue reading the second verse of Romans 12.

> *"Don't **copy** the behavior and customs of this world, but let God **transform** you into a new person by changing the way you **think**. Then you will learn to know God's will for you, which is good and pleasing and perfect."*
> Romans 12:2 NLT

This sounds a whole lot like what we have been studying in the previous chapters. The New Living Translation gives us further insight to Paul's words, and this gives us greater understanding. Let's look at the original Greek word used in this verse for *copy* (translated *conform* in the NKJV):

Syschematizo Greek: Compare to the English *scheme* and *schematic*. To fashion, to pattern or copy, to conform. This word refers to accommodating oneself to a model or pattern.

Gosh, that sure describes the way I lived for most of my life! I wanted to follow Jesus, however, the patterns and behaviors of the world were still seductive to me. I didn't want to be conformed to the world completely, but I did accommodate a part of myself to dabble in worldly ways and cares. Often this was not what we would consider sinful preoccupations, but what the world places emphasis on: such as appearance, education, position, celebrity, making our own way, and securing a future. These pursuits occupied a large part of my thinking as I related – not only to the world – but how I related to Jesus' church! I modeled parts of my life in the ways of the world, just as modeling clay wraps around an object to retain that object's image or when tracing-paper is used over a picture to make a nearly exact copy.

Slight Detour, Brain Patterns...

Now this gets really interesting.

The Lord God who made us and who knows us inside out has always known what neuroscience is just discovering: that when a person consistently thinks a certain way, the brain actually becomes patterned to default to these thought schematics which result in accompanying behavioral patterns.

Our brain is the most complex structure in the universe.[10] It is comprised of about 100 billion neurons that each have about 10,000 synapses that relate to other neurons. The function of our brain's neurons and synapses in how we live, communicate, process, and function are as varied as all of the stars in the galaxies and beyond. As I write this...I don't even understand it! However, these synapses grow with usage and can be molded to create *patterns* or familiar roadways, ruts, or grooves as we continue in a particular thought mode. What we see, sense, hear, smell, and touch can trigger old patterns of behavior without our being able to resist their onslaught.

This is a simplistic illustration, at best, to describe this incredible function of our brains, but let's use it as an example:

Randy and I just bought a new car. This new vehicle has its emergency brake on my right and my hand operates it. However, my brain has been programmed, as it were, over time to think that the emergency brake is on the floor, on my left as it was in my prior car. When I go to park the new car, I automatically find myself pushing on the floorboard with my left foot! I will need to intentionally stop and think about what I am doing. With practice and consistent usage to the new way of doing things, my reaction will be changed when I use the emergency brake in the new vehicle.

Now we can see one way that simple indulgences, that become more frequent to us, can become addictions or harmful behaviors *over time* as we allow the neurological pathways in our brain to become patterned after the ways of the world, let alone the devil's baits and hooks to turn us away from God.

God, however, created our brains. And, as we are learning, there is healing in Him. Our brains, neurons and synapses are amazingly flexible, and are constantly changing and rewiring. Having this little bit of information explains a lot.

In my story, when Jesus delivered me from the *root* of my depression and obsession with my appearance, which was a demonic oppression of pride, my thoughts – my brain – still needed to make new paths that no longer defaulted to old ways of thinking and behaving regarding food and my body. I was free from the enemy's grip, but transformation took place every time I moved a step forward (even when I'd fallen back several steps!) and made healthy choices.

Before that wonderful Saturday morning, the devil had the ability to "yank my chain." However, when his power was broken over me in Jesus Name, I was *free to choose* to decide to go the Lord's way and make new behaviors for my life. Before that time I didn't have the choice...*to choose*! With the power of the Holy Spirit and the authority of God's Word, new reactions, thoughts, and behaviors toward my appearance and my relationship with food were eventually completely transformed.

> *"And you He made alive, who were dead in trespasses and sins,*
> *in which you once walked according to the **course** of this world, **according to the prince of the power of the air**, the spirit who now works in the sons of disobedience,*
> *among whom also we all once conducted ourselves in the lusts of our flesh, **fulfilling the desires of the flesh and of the mind**, and were by nature children of wrath, just as the others*

> ***But God***, *who is rich in mercy, because of His great*
> *love with which He loved us..."*
> Ephesians 2:1-4

But God. What wonderful, marvelous, beyond comprehension words. Because of Him we no longer have to walk in the patterns of this world, the course of our enemy, and those of our own making.

We can be transformed.

Transformation...

Let's reread Romans 12:2 and continue on our journey forward:

> *"Don't **copy** the behavior and customs of this world,*
> *but let God **transform** you into a new person by*
> *changing the way you **think**. Then you will learn to*
> *know God's will for you, which is good and pleasing*
> *and perfect."*
> Romans 12:2 NLT

The original Greek for the word *transformed* speaks volumes to me:

Metamorphoo Greek: from the Greek ***meta*** denoting change of place or condition, and ***morphoo***, (English: *metamorphosis*), to form, to transform, transmute, change one's form; to alter fundamentally. Used of Jesus' transfiguration, which involved the miracle of transformation from an earthly form into a supernatural one.

It is fascinating to note that this word, ***metamorphoo***, has at its root the same prefix, ***meta***, *a change of place or condition* that the Greek word for *repentance,* ***metanoeo*** has. *Repentance* and *transformation* walk hand-in-hand!

Let's consider what areas of our thought lives we would most like to see transformation in and have freedom from constant struggle.

Below is a random list that may help:

- Fear(s)
- Unforgiveness towards someone
- Your past
- Being critical
- Past heartache
- Anger issues
- Depressing thoughts – occasional or continual discouragement
- Preoccupation about the future
- Divination – forecasting future conversations and circumstances
- Worry or anxiety
- Self-Pity
- "Beating yourself up" over what you say, do or how you appear
- Not measuring up
- Relationships
- Guilt
- Insecurity – a tendency to be over-sensitive to other's remarks, actions or non-actions
- Constantly comparing yourself to others
- Your appearance (this could be the way you look, your home, your family, your profession, etc.)
- Lust – in the broader sense of never being satisfied…with most anything in your life

- Sexual attractions outside of marriage: same sex, adulterous, promiscuous
- Struggle with any addiction
- Fantasy
- Needing to control
- Compulsion for information (ranging from personal circumstances or relationships to the world at large)
- Addictive behaviors – from food to prescription and non-prescription drugs (a preoccupation with the next *fix* or indulgence)
- Covetousness or envy
- Jealousy
- Not having the ability to trust a particular person or persons; unable to trust the Lord

The list could go on and on…however, there is no condemnation here. If you are identifying with anything from the list just given or if other troublesome areas of your life are coming to your mind, most likely these are areas the Holy Spirit is wanting to work on. He is desiring to pull some weeds so He can plant a lush and fruitful garden in your soul. The bottom line is – what is tripping you up?

If it is helpful to you, record below the three main areas of your thought life that you would like to have the Lord Jesus bring under His Lordship, even if you have surrendered these thought patterns to Him before:

- _____

- _____

- _____

Let's take a moment to specifically give these areas of our

thoughts to the Lord, and then let's receive the promise below:

> *"The LORD will guide you continually,*
> *And satisfy your **soul** (your heart and mind) in*
> *drought,*
> *And strengthen your bones;*
> *You shall be like a watered garden,*
> *And like a spring of water, whose waters do not*
> *fail."*
> Isa 58:11 (Parentheses, mine)

He is already at work on these deeply felt needs that you have. Even if you have barely begun to surrender these deep places in your soul to Him, Jesus has them in His loving and healing hands.[11]

At one point, when I finally confessed to my husband the stranglehold that fantasy had on my life, I remember telling him I was terrified that I would feel a great emptiness if Jesus *did* release me from this stronghold! I felt like an alcoholic trying to take his last drink – what would replace the time and effort spent on the addiction? What thoughts and activities would take the place of my daydreams? Real life would seem so mundane and unfulfilling in comparison with the great exploits that I could imagine. (By the grace of God alone, my husband stayed loving and committed to me after I said that to him!).

However, that confession was a part of my first *layers* of surrender (and again, repentance), which loosened the enemy's lying grip. And what a liar the devil is! I have found that his fantasies, seductions, and temptations I fell prey to are like empty ashes compared to the exhilaration, vitality, and joy of experiencing life in the Holy Spirit...in *reality*. From my personal experience, *real life* in God surpasses any *altered* state of reality (what fantasy and substance abuse are) no matter if I am washing the dishes, sitting at my desk at work or having a fabulous ministry opportunity in another country! As noted author and speaker Beth Moore often states, "There is no high like the Most High!"

I pray that you find encouragement from my experience to not give up when complete freedom doesn't take place with the snap of your fingers.[12] You are learning to surrender and make a U-turns from the frailty of your "old-man," and are beginning to walk in the newness of your mind and life in Christ.[13]

Renewal...

It is so helpful to read the Bible using various translations. God's Word is like a multi-faceted diamond. You may be looking at the gemstone (a particular verse) in your hands, but as you turn it to the scrutiny and light of different translations from the original Hebrew of the Old Testament and from the original Greek of the New Testament, you can gain a greater grasp of the beauty of the original wording. Let's read Romans 12:2 again, this time from the New King James Version:

> *"And do not be conformed to this world, but be transformed by the **renewing** of your mind, that you may prove what is that good and acceptable and perfect will of God."*

Here we find that our minds are not only changed, as the New Living Translation informed us, but they are *renewed...*

Anakainosis Greek: To renew, renewal, renovation, rejuvenation, the process and work of restoring something back to a *new* condition.

Please tell me which of those word or phrase definitions you *don't* like! Oh my; every one of them is wondrous, beautiful, and filled with hope. The Holy Spirit would not have penned these words through Paul if they were not His intent and purpose for your life. Anything less is less than all God has for you.

I want to take a moment to encourage you to believe that *refreshing, restoration,* and *renewal* are yours as a child of God. It is time to *believe* His Word. As noted author and speaker Beth Moore often states, "It is easy to believe in God, but do you *believe Him*?" She then challenges us further:

> *"After all…If believers don't believe, what on earth do they do?"*[14]

That line makes me laugh…except that I have found it to be so true! However, it *is* easier to doubt Jesus' love for us and His power within us by the Holy Spirit. It *is* so easy for us to default to what we know is comfortable. Maybe we have been previously disappointed when we didn't see transformation immediately. There may be a variety of reasons for this, however, I believe the Lord is challenging some of us make the choice to *believe* Him *again*; to really grab hold of the truth that He is *not* finished with us, and that He has so much more for us to experience in Him…renewal, renovation, and rejuvenation!

Walking in His Will...

One of the great reasons and benefits for the Holy Spirit's transforming work in our thoughts is the ability to better discern the will of God for our lives as *Romans 12:2* states. Who doesn't want to be able to do this? Let's read this verse one final time, below:

> *"Don't copy the behavior and customs of this world,*

*but let God **transform** you into a new person by changing the way you **think**. Then you will learn **to know God's will for you**, which is good and pleasing and perfect."*
Romans 12:2 NLT

I have spent countless years struggling to discern Jesus' plans for my life. Now, as I try daily (again, I'm still in process) to pour out my agenda for the Lord's agenda, my first-love passion for Him has been restored. Not only that, but I seem to be experiencing greater clarity of what He is up to in my life, my family, and my ministry along with greater clarity to be able *to choose* the Holy Spirit's direction. Knowing God's will no longer seems to be the mystery it once was to me. What a rich and unexpected blessing! What overwhelming satisfaction in His love alone. I'm more apt to be in the right place at the right time when I let the Holy Spirit guide my steps, whether big or small.

Hmmmm....It's like a veil has been lifted from over my mind...

"Whom have I in heaven but You? And there is none upon earth that I desire besides You.
My flesh and my heart fail; But God is the strength of my heart and my portion forever."
Psalms 73:25-26

Study Questions...

- Did you find surrendering your life to the Lord Jesus difficult? Why do you think that was? (It is often helpful recognize the *fear factor* that hinders us.)

- In your own words, why is it *not* beneficial for us to copy the ways and thoughts of the world?

- Re-read the definition of the Greek word used for *transformation* that is found in this chapter. What encourages you most from the definition?

- Was it helpful to read the list of possiblethought patterns that trip-up our lives? How do you think your life would be different if the thought patterns you identified with were transformed by the Lord?

- If you have been encouraged by studying Romans 12:1-2, explain what you are sensing the Lord is speaking to you.

---

[1] 1 John 2:15

[2] Isaiah 43:10, John 17:3

[3] Luke 9:23-24

[4] Luke 8:8

[5] Psalm 103:11-14

[6] Psalm 139:1-13

[7] Psalm 103:13-14

[8] Hebrews 4:16

[9] Psalm 62:8

[10] Frank Amthor, Neuroscience for Dummies (http://www.dummies.com/how-to/content/neuroscience-for-dummies-cheat-sheet.html) John Wiley & Sons, Inc.

[11] Psalm 27:14, Psalm 55:22, Luke 12:22, Philippians 4:6, Hebrews 13:5-6

[12] Hebrews 10:35-36

[13] Ephesians 4:20-24

[14] Beth Moore, *Praying God's Word* (Nashville, TN: B & H Publishers, 2000)

Living In a New Kingdom

"For He has rescued us from the dominion of darkness and brought us into the kingdom of the Son He loves,"
Colossians 1:13 NIV

We will now take a look at a beautiful prayer that Paul prays for the church in Colossae that has been handed down to us to be our petition.

Fruitful Lives...

His Spirit-breathed prayer reveals God's heart for His children: that we would know Him intimately and bear lush fruit for His glory.[1] This is what walking in the Spirit looks like:

> *"For this reason we also, since the day we heard it, do not cease to pray for you, and to ask that you may be filled with the knowledge of His will in all wisdom and spiritual understanding;*
> *that you may walk worthy of the Lord, fully pleasing Him, being fruitful in every good work and increasing*

in the knowledge of God;"
Colossians 1:9-10

At the outset of His prayer, Paul is reminding us to live lives worthy of the Lord. What does that look like? It has a lot to do with what we discussed in the previous chapter:

Sweet surrender – my weeds for His lush garden in my life
    Discovering His will for my daily life
        Bringing delight to His heart

Being exceedingly fruitful – abundance for myself and for others
    Knowing Him intimately – in continually greater measure
        Having spiritual understanding – who I am in Him

Paul then prays that we be…

> *"...strengthened with all might, according to His glorious power, for all patience and longsuffering with joy;*
>   *giving thanks to the Father who has qualified us to be partakers of the inheritance of the saints in the light."*
> Colossians 1:11-12

Whew! This is powerful stuff that Paul is requesting here! If you tag team this prayer with his prayer found in Ephesians 1, we learn that Paul desires we be strengthened with might through the Holy Spirit in the inner man (our souls and spirits). Sign me up!

Why is this inner strengthening so important? We find the answer in the next phrase, *"for all patience and longsuffering with joy."*

Patience and *longsuffering* don't seem to fit together with the word *joy*. These two words seem like polar opposites; however, they reveal the abundant life that Jesus promises. This is a life not dependent upon circumstances dictating our emotions, but a life relying solely in the power and joy of the Holy Spirit to face anything that comes our way.[2] For the joy set before Him, Jesus endured the cross – a paradox if there ever was one.[3]

Just one hour ago, I learned that a member of the church family my husband and I pastor had just been celebrating her son's second birthday with her family. Suddenly, her father collapsed and passed from this life into the throne room of the King. This is where the rubber-of-the-road of life collides with the reality of the truth of God's Word and power. This is where mental theory of the Christian life doesn't cut it, but where the genuine *experience* of the comfort, help, strength, and joy that the Holy Spirit can give is all-sustaining. We don't want anything cluttering up the Spirit's beyond-reason ability to provide all that we need...and then some...especially when sadness and tragedy strike.

I found this to be absolutely true and trustworthy when diagnosed with Stage 4 incurable cancer a few years ago! The tangible joy and happiness of the Holy Spirit was my rock to stand on. This joy has been a greater testimony than that of the physical touch from the Lord that has kept me alive these past several years – *years* past my prognosis' expiration date!

The Devil's Darkness...

Next is the portion of Paul's prayer that I want to focus on:

> *"He has **delivered** us from the **power** of **darkness** and conveyed us into the kingdom of the Son of His love,*

> *in whom we have redemption through His*
> *blood, the forgiveness of sins."*
> Colossians 1:13-14

This part of Paul's prayer is music to our soul! Let's take a few moments to open this passage up to revel in a glimpse of its meaning.

For Jesus has **delivered**...

Rhyomai Greek: To draw or snatch from danger, rescue, deliver.[4]

Jesus already *delivered* us from the **power** ...

Exousia Greek: Something that is permissible, allowed, permission, authority to do something. It is not only the capability to do something, but the right and authority to carry out the action. That which is subject to one's rule, dominion or jurisdiction. The power to do as one pleases. The power over persons and things.[5]

He has delivered us from the power of **darkness**...

Skotos Greek: From the root word "*ska*" to cover. The word is literally used for physical darkness, and metaphorically used for spiritual, moral, and intellectual darkness. A shadow caused by intercepting light. Darkness arising from error, ignorance, disobedience, willful blindness, and rebellion. Darkness is an evil system absolutely opposed to the light.[6]

Why is this important to know? Because we need to realize that when Adam and Eve disobeyed God in the Garden of Eden, they not only died spiritually; they also handed over their entire God-given dominion[7] of this planet to the devil. Their bite into the little piece of forbidden fruit caused hell to be unleashed on Earth because of the transfer of power from their hands over to the prince of all evil.[8]

Jesus never disputed the enemy's right to rule this planet when He was tempted by the adversary in the wilderness.[9] Satan had the authority to give all the kingdoms of this world to Jesus if He would take his shortcut and bypass the horrific cross of Calvary for our redemption. Jesus calls this king of darkness, *the ruler of this world*.[10]

How dark is the adversary's darkness! With his evil deceptions he blinds and covers (Greek: *ska*) men's hearts and minds[11] from the knowledge of the Truth.[12] His deceptions and lies continue to this day; indeed, they are his very nature. Jesus calls him the father of lies.[13] If you have ever wondered about the evil in the world, here is your answer: The enemy has full reign and control. Yet don't be alarmed – sobered, yes – but not alarmed. Though the devil may be mighty, our God is ALMIGHTY!

Time to Celebrate...

> *"And now I have told you before it comes, that when it does come to pass, you may believe.*
> *I will no longer talk much with you, for the ruler of this world is coming, **and he has nothing in Me.***"
> John 14:29-30

What cause for celebration! What understanding it brings to the portion of the Lord's Prayer, "Your kingdom come, Your will be done!"[14] That is not a passive stance, but a bold declaration that in Jesus' name[15] the believer can take back authority over the kingdom of darkness by enforcing the rule of heaven. This right of dominion is due to us because we are children of the true King, and we are hidden in Him.[16] Our enemy, now a toothless lion (though he can still roar loudly),[17] was stripped of his power and weaponry at the cross.[18]

Oh! To live in this truth from God's Word! This knowledge is one of the reasons why we need a transformation in our mind and heart. We need to be truly able to see, feel, and understand the circumstances of our life *and* the world around us for what they really are.[19]

We will not see the full restoration of the Kingdom of God until Jesus' return.[20] Yet in the meantime, we are learning that the battles we wage on Earth are not with people, but with demonic beings[21] whose mission is to rob, kill, and destroy God's treasured humanity as we read in John 10:10.

A New Location...

However, we have great news! We have already been ***conveyed*** or ***transferred*** from this evil ruler's kingdom of darkness...

Methistemi Greek: From the same root as *transformed* and *repent*; ***meta***. Literally, "to set aside." The word indicates a change from one place to another, a removal, a transfer or a relocation. A change of situation.[22]

How many of us could use a change in location or situation? Yikes! That sounds awesome! So if this is true, where have we been transferred to? *The **kingdom** of the Son He **loves**...*

Basileia Greek: Royal dominion, kingdom, realm of rule, the exercise of dominion.[23]

Agape Greek: To love, cherish, esteem, favor, honor, respect, accept, prize, relish; to be devoted to. *Agape* denotes an undefeatable benevolence and unconquerable good will that always seeks the highest good of the other person, no matter what he does. It is the self-giving love that gives freely without asking anything in return and does not consider the worth of its object. *Agape* is more a love by choice than by chance. *Agape* describes the unconditional love God has for the world.[24]

In my darkest hours I almost always had the thought, "If I could only just run away!" I would either blame my circumstances or think the grass looked greener elsewhere. The trouble with this line of thinking – though I didn't realize it then – is that I really wanted to run away from *myself*. Wherever I would have gone, I would have taken *me* along!

The wonder-filled news is that in Christ Jesus, you and I have already experienced an amazing *change in location*. The wording is all past tense: We have already been *transferred* and *relocated*. Where? We now live in the royal realm and rule of the Beloved Son. No kingdom on earth can compare with this royal dominion whose King is no less than God Himself; the Lord Jesus Christ. And, how does this King rule? With undefeatable benevolence and unconquerable goodwill; with unfailing love that esteems, honors, favors, respects, and prizes His beloved sons and daughters.

Living in Love's Kingdom...

As God's cherished children we have an immense spiritual inheritance that is not only our gift as we enter heaven's gates, but is *already* our spiritual possession while we still walk planet Earth. We have been positioned with Jesus in heavenly places – the spiritual realm.[25] We are already living eternally in the Kingdom of the Son of God's Love.[26] Though we are not studying these truths in depth in this book, this glimpse of who we are in Him compels each one of us to search the Scriptures for greater understanding for ourselves. This was

Paul's prayer for us.[27]

I love to recall the story of the Old Testament prophet Elisha, found in 2 Kings 6:8-23. If you have never read it, you are in for a treat – it is a hoot!

When Elisha and his servant were surrounded on every side by the Syrian army that was set to destroy them, Elisha prayed that his servant's eyes would be opened to reveal what was really going on. Yes, the enemy's presence was near and fierce; but the servant began to see the true reality of their circumstances. He saw the hosts of the Army of God surrounding the enemy with heavenly horses and chariots of fire that were even greater. We are more than conquerors through Him who loves us![28]

The early disciples of Christ walked in Jesus' authority as they not only preached the gospel, but demonstrated its power through the Holy Spirit. Nothing has changed.[29] The Lord Jesus has given us authority over the king of darkness and his demonic hordes.[30] We have this authority because of the shed blood of Jesus on the cross. We have the complete and total, once and for all forgiveness of our sin;[31] and we are raised up and positioned with Him in heavenly places.[32]

You are probably realizing what ramifications our knowledge about the Kingdom we are truly living in has on our thought lives. Here we understand Paul's call to us through the ages: to not have our thinking be patterned after the world's way of thinking, which is subject to the ruler of darkness. We used to live there, but we *now* have a new zip code. We are living in the Kingdom of Jesus' marvelous *agape* for us.

Let's leave the clutter of our old way of thinking about life behind, and have our eyes opened to see what the Holy Spirit is doing all around us: in our homes, our schools, our workplaces, our nation, our world…everywhere we set foot! What adventure, refreshment, and purpose await us as our King transforms and heals our hearts and minds.

Let's press on!

"…the eyes of your understanding being enlightened; that you may know what is the hope of His calling, what are the riches of the glory of His inheritance in the saints,

and what is the exceeding greatness of His power toward us who believe, according to the working of His mighty power…"
Ephesians 1:18-19

Study Questions...

- What does it mean for you to have a fruitful life?

- What does the word *rescue* mean to you? What has the Lord already rescued you from, and what other areas of your life still need His rescue?

- Does knowing that Jesus has already transferred you into His Kingdom of love help you in your current circumstances? Explain.

- Look back at the definition of God's love, *agape*. What words or phrases were most meaningful to you from the definition and why?

- What are your thoughts concerning our God-given authority over our adversary, the devil?

[1] John 15:8

[2] Nehemiah 8:10

[3] Hebrews 12:2

[4] Spiros Zodhiates, Th.D., Executive Editor, *The Key Word Study Bible*. New International Version (Chatanooga, TN: AMG Publishers. 1996).

[5] Ibid.

[6] Jack W. Hayford, Sr. Editor, *New Spirit Filled Life Bible*, New King James Version (Nashville, TN: Thomas Nelson, Inc., 2002), *Word Wealth*. Luke 11:35

[7] Genesis 1:26

[8] Genesis 2:17, Genesis 3:1-7

[9] Matthew 4:1-11, Luke 4:1-13

[10] John 12:31, John 14:30, John 16:11

[11] Ephesians 2:2-3

[12] John 14:6

[13] John 8:44

[14] Matthew 6:10, Luke 11:2

[15] Acts 3:6,16

[16] Colossians 3:3

[17] 1 Peter 5:8

[18] Colossians 2:14-15

[19] 2 Corinthians 5:7

[20] Matthew 14:27

[21] Ephesians 6:12

[22] Jack W. Hayford, Sr. Editor, *New Spirit Filled Life Bible*, New King James Version (Nashville, TN: Thomas Nelson, Inc., 2002), *Word Wealth*. Luke 11:35
Blue Letter Bible: http//www.blueletterbible.org/

[23] Spiros Zodhiates, Th.D., Executive Editor, *The Key Word Study Bible*. New International Version (Chatanooga, TN: AMG Publishers. 1996).

[24] Ibid.

Jack W. Hayford, Sr. Editor, *New Spirit Filled Life Bible*, New King James Version (Nashville, TN: Thomas Nelson, Inc., 2002), *Word Wealth*. Luke 11:35

[25] Ephesians 2:4-10

[26] John 17:3

[27] Ephesians 1:18

[28] Romans 8:37

[29] Hebrews 13:8

[30] Luke 10:17-20

[31] Hebrews 9:12, Hebrews 10:10

[32] Colossians 2:13, Ephesians 2:4-8

Lifting Our Veil

*"Now the Lord is the Spirit; and **where the Spirit of the Lord is, there is liberty**.*

*But we all, with **unveiled face**, beholding as in a mirror the glory of the Lord, are being transformed into the same image from glory to glory, just as by the Spirit of the Lord."*
2 Corinthians 3:17-18

Let's have a little "refresher!"

The Greek word *skotos*, translated *darkness* – as in the kingdom we were once in slavery to – has as its root the Greek word *ska*, meaning *to cover*. The remainder of the translation of *skotos* is *a shadow caused by intercepting light; a darkness arising from error, ignorance, disobedience, willful blindness, and rebellion.*

A Veil of Darkness...

What comes to your mind when you think of not being able to *see* because there is something covering your eyes, both spiritually and physically?

Paul tells us that before Christ entered our lives, our minds were covered by a *veil.*

> *"But even if our gospel is **veiled**, it is **veiled** to those who are perishing,*
>
> *whose **minds** the god of this age has blinded, who do not believe, lest the light of the gospel of the glory of Christ, who is the image of God, should shine on them."*
> 2 Corinthians 4:3-4

Before our receiving the Lord personally into our lives by faith, our spirits were not only without life, but our minds were covered by a *veil of darkness* from the god of this age (the devil). We truly walked without seeing, blindly being led by the enemy of our hearts. But praise be to God, light always overpowers darkness…

> *"For we do not preach ourselves, but Christ Jesus the Lord, and ourselves your bondservants for Jesus' sake.*
>
> *For it is the God who commanded light to shine out of darkness, who has shone in **our hearts** to give the **light** of the knowledge of the glory of God in the face of Jesus Christ."*
> 2 Corinthians 4:5-6

For God so loved us that He commanded His light to shine into the veiled darkness of our minds and hearts. Our choice to receive His mercy and grace transferred our spiritual location from the kingdom of darkness to the Kingdom of His agape love. As an added bonus, the veil that once shrouded our minds from God's light was ripped away!

Paul explains this earlier in his letter to the Corinthians regarding Jews who had not yet recognized Jesus as the long-awaited Messiah.

This passage relates to us as well:

> *"But their **minds were blinded**. For until this day the same **veil** remains unlifted in the reading of the Old Testament, **because the veil is taken away in Christ**.*
>
> *But even to this day, when Moses is read, a veil lies on their heart."*
> 2 Corinthians 3:14-15

Now, it gets really exciting!

> *"Nevertheless when one turns to the Lord, **the veil is taken away**.*
>
> *Now the Lord is the Spirit; and **where the Spirit of the Lord is, there is liberty**.*
>
> *But we all, with **unveiled face**, beholding as in a mirror the glory of the Lord, are being transformed into the same image from glory to glory, just as by the Spirit of the Lord."*
> 2 Corinthians 3:16-18

This unveiling is very much a picture of a beautiful, precious, much beloved bride walking toward her Groom. Her face is veiled (okay, this is how we "older" brides used to wear them!). When it is time for the announcement of marriage, the Groom lifts the bride's veil so they both may see each other without hindrance. What an exquisite analogy of what took place for us when we were born again in the Spirit!

The veil we wore over our minds and hearts before coming to Christ *was not* the lovely, white-lace, delicate adornment that a bride would wear. The veil we wore was tattered, soiled, gross, ugly, and so dense that we couldn't navigate life. *Repentance*, the surrender of our thoughts for God's thoughts, lifted the devil's ugly, weighty headpiece.

Jesus has removed the veil separating us from God's light. This is much like the rending of the veil in the Jerusalem temple when Jesus died.[1] That torn piece of dense, heavy fabric signified that anyone who received God's forgiveness through Christ could now stand in the Holy of Holies of God's presence. Now, we too, have had the veil torn off from our souls, and we can behold His glorious light and experience times of healing and liberating refreshment in the liberty of the Holy Spirit.

Still we struggle. The Spirit's breath into our dark spirits and His light shining into our souls can be difficult to reconcile when we continue to have such tremendous battles in our thoughts. How does this knowledge about the veil help us to live as Christians? We still *physically* live in the enemy's kingdom. How do we grow in walking in the Holy Spirit's freedom? Why do our thoughts *and* emotions trip us up so often?

This is where the god of this world still has influence in what we perceive in our thoughts. He would like to keep the old veil over our minds and hearts – our ***souls***.

Tempting Thoughts are not Sin...

Remember our spirit is filled with the Holy Spirit, but our soul is still a work in progress. This side of heaven, our sin-nature and the weakness of our flesh are vulnerable to enticement away from God. There remains the minute-by-minute choice for us to walk in the flesh or in the power of the Holy Spirit.[2] And, the enemy still has the ability to tempt us.

Where do these temptations first take place? Yes, in our *thoughts*. This is where I became stalled in my life; experiencing more bondage than liberty, defeat instead of victory.

One major hurdle to my personal freedom was the long-held notion that every thought passing through my mind must be *my* thought. Even thoughts enticing me into temptation. Gosh, these thoughts sure *sounded* like me!

I had been taught and read in God's Word that **to be tempted is not sin**. It is the *choice* I make with temptation that determines victory or defeat, but to be tempted in the first place **is not sin**. Jesus was my example. The spotless Lamb of God was tempted in every way possible that we humans are tempted, yet these temptations He faced where never considered sin in themselves. The Bible clearly tells us He did not sin. When He was tempted by Satan and resisted the enemy's seductions, Jesus did not yield to him and was victorious.[3]

Through His victory over temptation, we find the strength of the Holy Spirit to overcome as well. Still, I believed that whenever I had a sinful or ungodly thought (four million times a day, I might add), I figured *I had already sinned* because I had the thought in the first place! Because these tempting thoughts sure sounded like my voice in my head, **they must be *my* thoughts!**

It wasn't until, by the grace of God, I realized these initial tempting thoughts become sin *only* when I entertain them or give them a place to continue in my mind. Only when I linger in these thoughts do I stumble into sin – missing the mark of God's holiness. **The thoughts themselves are not sin.** Yes my flesh *may* want to indulge in a tempting activity, but if I *resist* the thought of temptation (no matter whether it originates from the enemy *or* myself) I have chosen the path of freedom and of not failure.

Duh, that's a no-brainer. Most of us have been taught this truth. Yet, I have prayed with countless Christians who get tripped up in their minds with no relief from constant struggle and guilt over their *thoughts of temptation*. They know the truth about temptation alone not being sin. Yet, because the ugly thoughts sound like their voice or because these temptations seem to originate in *their* mind, they believe they *must be* their desires. They are convinced they have already fallen into sin by simply having the thoughts. This is not the truth of God's Word.[4]

James, the Lord's brother and the pastor of the early church in Jerusalem, explains the process of temptation. He gives us a great promise when we resist tempting thoughts and a great consequence when we don't:

> *"Blessed is the man who endures temptation; for when he has been approved, he will receive the crown of life which the Lord has promised to those who love Him.*
>
> *Let no one say when he is tempted, "I am tempted by God"; for God cannot be tempted by evil, nor does He Himself tempt anyone.*
>
> *But each one is tempted when he is drawn away by his own desires and enticed.*
>
> *Then, when desire has conceived, it gives birth to sin; and sin, when it is full-grown, brings forth death."*
> James 1:12-15

Temptation comes from the great tempter – the devil[5] – and, yes, our own flesh is enticed by sin. Nevertheless, we can refuse to harbor, nurture, and entertain these thoughts so they do not birth and grow into sinful thoughts or actions. Popular author and speaker Joyce Meyer hit the nail on the head when she termed these thought cycles *"The Battlefield of the Mind."*

Because of the enemy's access to our thoughts and his ability to deceive and seduce us, we see even further that we must carefully *guard* both our minds and our hearts. We are already tempted enough without adding undue exposure to ourselves with harmful influences such as inappropriate media, music, reading material, unhealthy relationships or placing ourselves in potentially dark and tempting situations.[6]

Resisting = Transformation...

We find great help from the Scriptures. The Holy Spirit inspired Paul to give us a detailed litmus test to help us determine whose thoughts are flickering across our minds. All thoughts coming from the Lord Jesus Christ look like the following:

> *"Finally, brethren, whatever things are true, whatever things are noble, whatever things are just, whatever things are pure, whatever things are lovely, whatever things are of good report, if there is any virtue and if there is anything praiseworthy -- **meditate** (or think) on these things."*
> Philippians 4:8 (Parentheses, mine)

James also gives us pointers as to what characterizes the Lord's thinking:

> *"**Do not be deceived**, my beloved brethren.*
> *Every good gift and every perfect gift is from above, and comes down from the Father of lights, with whom there is no variation or shadow of turning."*
> James 1:16-17

> *"But the wisdom that is from above is first pure,*

96

then peaceable, gentle, willing to yield, full of mercy
and good fruits, without partiality and without
hypocrisy."
James 3:17

We see Jesus in every word we just read. His thoughts are noble, just, pure, lovely, of good report, virtuous, praiseworthy, and they bring God's peace. Everything that is good and perfect comes from the Father of all light in whom there is no darkness at all. Jesus speaks purity, peace, and mercy that encourage the fruit of the Holy Spirit in our lives.

On the other hand, the enemy's thoughts in our minds sound like this:

"But if you have bitter envy and self-seeking in your
hearts, do not boast and lie against the truth.
This wisdom does not descend from above, but is
earthly, sensual, demonic.
For where envy and self-seeking exist, confusion and
every evil thing are there."
James 3:14-16

If a thought enters my mind and it doesn't match the Lord's list of characteristics, I know it is not from Him. If I know it is a thought *I don't want to think* either, even though it may sound like my voice, *I **don't have to continue thinking it**.* Jesus has lifted the veil that once blinded my mind, and I can now *choose* to walk in His liberty.

The previous paragraph is the whole purpose for writing this little book. Please, read it again and take some time to ponder what these words may mean to you.

This is what it means to be transformed by the renewing our

minds that we read previously in Romans 12:2. ***Transformation is this simple***. When I begin the practice of resisting tempting, ungodly, negative thoughts: slowly, but surely, I am being transformed into the image of Jesus.

Granted, starting to live this way may be a battle. We have many thought patterns we immediately default to because we have been thinking them over a long period of time. This is particularly true for thoughts that have found their way into our emotions. Many of these thoughts have become our identity, but that is not the truth!

Especially at first, we may win some thought battles and we may lose some thought battles. When the enemy recognizes we are becoming a threat to his diminished kingdom of darkness, he may pull out his heavy artillery. However, his weapons are no match for the power of the Lord Jesus![7] The Bible tells us that the Lord stripped the enemy of his ammunition, so do not become discouraged with these tug-of-wars that Peter talked about.[8] As we move forward in resisting thoughts that the Lord doesn't want us to have and we don't want to have, we see that the Lord always provides a way of escape for us to flee these temptations.[9] Progressively, the Spirit's winning advance in our lives will become more frequent. How He does this is one of the ways we become attuned to His leading.

Paul is spot-on about what we have been learning when he gives us specific instructions for when unwanted thoughts come our way:

> *"For though we walk in the flesh, we do not war according to the flesh.*
> *For the weapons of our warfare are not carnal but mighty in God for pulling down strongholds,*
> *casting down arguments and every high thing that exalts itself against the knowledge of God, **bringing every thought into captivity to the obedience of***

Christ,"
2 Corinthians 10:3-5

Bringing our thoughts captive to Jesus means bringing the ugly thoughts we have and exchanging them for what is noble, pure, and lovely. This truth greatly affects our lives. From personal experience I can tell you that my joy and happiness quotient goes through the roof when I am consistently living in the verse we read. In truth, we are actually engaging in spiritual warfare and turning the enemy on his head in our minds, hearts, lives, and situations when we choose to bring our thoughts captive to the Lord.

How many decades I was loaded with guilt because of my thoughts!

I lived under a lie that when I experienced tempting thoughts I had already sinned and it was too late. I reasoned that because *I* had the tempting thought, I must really want to do it. I was shot down before I could even make the right choice not to harbor the temptation. I had played right into the enemy's hands.

Keeping the Veil Lifted...

Glory!! Yippee!! Hallelujah!! The veil has been lifted! If a thought comes to me and I know it is not from the Lord of love (because the Bible clearly tells me how He thinks) and I don't want to hold onto it: *I don't have to agree with it, own it, partner with it or give place to it.*

I literally say these phrases to my thoughts! If I am tempted to be critical of someone I simply say or think, "I'm not receiving that!" If I am tempted to be drawn into a fantasy world, as I still randomly am at times, I say to that tempting thought, "I'm not agreeing with you!"

99

or, "I'm not going there!" If a thought comes that will undermine my faith, I quote Scriptures and resist the devil who is trying to make me doubt.

As author Neil Anderson writes in *The Bondage Breaker*:

> *"You don't have to out-shout him or out-muscle him to be free of his influence. Believe, declare, and act upon the truth of God's Word and you will thwart Satan's strategy."*

Should I fall and let myself entertain tempting thoughts or even act out in sin, I no longer partner with the enemy who would try to flood me with guilt. I come to the Lord who has already forgiven me, and I no longer have to live in condemnation![10] I ask Jesus to continue His cleansing work in my life. I then resist the guilty thoughts that often come from the accuser during times like these. I know guilt is not from the Lord, and I sure don't want to labor under guilt either! This is a choice for us to believe the truth of God's Word over the lies of the enemy. What impetus this gives us to really know the Bible for ourselves!

Through the power of the Holy Spirit who lives in me, I am slowly (I emphasize, s-l-o-w-l-y) learning to bring all of my thoughts captive to the obedience of Christ who is the Lord of all joy, peace, life, and light.[11] I get a chance to partner with the Holy Spirit a zillion times a day to renew my mind from the old critical, selfish, self-absorbed "Sue" way of thinking into what Jesus would have me think – which is a whole lot more happy, fulfilling, and exciting!

Our ability to do this may be halting at first, and it may take some time before we start seeing more successes than failures; however, these are the steps of genuine repentance we have been learning about. Developing a new way of thinking – God's way of thinking takes time

– and let's face it, we've been partnering with some of these thought-ruts a really l-o-n-g time. Some of these ruts are so deep that when we look up from their depths, our eyes aren't even at street-level! Every time we rely on the Holy Spirit to resist tempting thoughts, no matter what they are, the Lord is re-routing and renewing our brain patterns.

Examples...

For years I "beat myself up" over every sin, failure, and misstep I thought I had made:

"Oh! Why did I say that?"
"Why did I do that?"
"Why did I blow it…again!!"
"Why can't I be different?"

I was so tired and weary of always feeling badly about myself. Does anybody know what I'm talking about?

One evening after a barrage of "why did I" questions, I sensed the Lord giving me a picture in my mind:

I saw a table stacked with dirty, yucky, caked-on-food dishes that were piled high – as if someone had left a huge mess on a dining room table. From out of nowhere I saw the white-robed arm of the Lord swiping those dishes off the table until all that remained was the clean, white, linen tablecloth underneath – pure and pristine.

I knew He was giving me a picture of my mind and the years of "why did I's." Each thought was all piled up, plate-upon-plate, useless and dirty. In that instant I knew I was never to think that way again about myself.

When those thoughts of feeling bad about myself come on

occasion, like a glancing tap on the shoulder and not a brick to my head as they used to come, I "see" His arm making a clean slate of that table. I know these accusations are not from the Lord Jesus and I know I don't want them. I simply don't receive them or give them a place to taunt me anymore.

I cannot begin to express how this has freed me from mental torment. It also has allowed the Holy Spirit to actually go deeper in my soul to heal the real insecurities and behaviors that once held me. Because I've stopped listening to the noisy, condemning voices of my flesh and the enemy, I now have more clarity and discernment to hear the Spirit's voice.

I used to be a very critical person. Now I am a *not so* critical person. I am definitely a work in progress! In my workplace I was tempted to think some sour thoughts towards a new employee who was bringing a lot of grief to me personally as she was a professing atheist and hostile toward Christianity. At times, her conversation was laced in sexual innuendo with religious overtones. Critical thoughts abounded in my mind and gossip was on my tongue. Bummer. Yes it was true that it was challenging to work with her, but I knew the Lord wasn't pleased with the agreements I was making with these joy-robbing thoughts. Ouch! I should have known better; being critical and having the joy of the Lord at the same time is pretty much impossible.

I knew the thoughts popping into my head were not noble, pure, or lovely as Philippians 4:8 teaches. They certainly were not God's thoughts towards this co-worker, and I didn't want to continue thinking this way either. I asked for the Lord's help to bring my negative thoughts captive to the love of Jesus and exchange what I was allowing for His heart toward her. When a critical thought would come, I'd think instead, "I don't receive this" or "I'm not going there" or "I don't have to do this...Lord I want Your thoughts toward her."

Soon I began sensing the Spirit's leading regarding how to genuinely care for this woman and share His love for her. I had the great privilege of seeing her come to Christ and she is one of my dearest friends today.

Granted, many of us have strongholds – something that has a strong *hold* on us – where we have allowed the devil to gain so much ground in our hearts and minds we genuinely need the delivering power of the Lord Jesus.[12] Resisting alone is unable to keep us from spiraling into thoughts and behaviors that we detest and prevent us from glorifying the Lord we love so much. We will look at some Scriptural help for these areas in our lives in the next chapter. However, as we choose to believe what God's Word tells us about the uncovering of the enemy's veil from our minds, and as we intentionally begin to recognize the source of many of our thoughts: real, lasting and profound *refreshing*, *restoration* and *renewal*, will take place in our lives, full of all the fruit and the gifts of the Holy Spirit.

Can you think of anything more wonderful?

> *"Therefore, if anyone is in Christ, he is a new creation; old things have passed away; behold, all things have become new."*
> 2 Corinthians 5:17

Study Questions...

- How did learning from the Scriptures about the enemy's veil over your mind speak to you?

- How does knowing that you no longer have to live under the veil of the enemy touch your heart?

- Can you think of some practical things you can do that might help curb the world's influence on your thoughts?

- Explain how bringing every thought captive to the Lord of love could bring transformation to your life?

- Do you have any recurring thoughts that are like "dirty dishes?" Are you now more hopeful for the Lord's transformation in this area of your life? Explain.

[1] Mark 15:38

[2] Galatians 5:16-18

[3] Hebrews 4:14-15

[4] Hebrews 4:14-15 added again for emphasis of this truth!

[5] Luke 4:1-13

[6] Psalm 101:2-4, 1 Peter 1:13-16, 1 Peter 5:8

[7] Colossians 2:14-15

[8] 1 Peter 1:13-15

[9] 1 Corinthians 10:13

[10] Romans 8:1

[11] 2 Corinthians 10:3-5

[12] 2 Corinthians 10:4, Luke 11:19-23

Untying the Knots

"The Spirit of the Lord GOD is upon Me,
Because the LORD has anointed Me
To preach good tidings to the poor;
He has sent Me to heal the brokenhearted,
To proclaim liberty to the captives,
And the opening of the prison to those who are bound;"
Isa 61:1

When we first came to faith in the saving grace of the Lord Jesus Christ, each of saw an immediate difference in our lives for the better.

Hope! Joy! Forgiveness! A fresh clean start! Some of us have had such radical transformation experiences the world around took notice. Others of us may not have a dramatic conversion story to tell, yet we know we are indescribably different from the inside out. Our lives have been irrevocably changed by the power of the gospel – or good news – of Jesus' rescue mission for us personally.[1]

Nevertheless, maybe a few years down the road on our walk with the Lord, we now seem to find ourselves in the same predicament Paul found himself in of "doing things he didn't want to do and not doing what he should."[2]

Try as we might, we can't seem to resist or break free from thoughts, behaviors, or long held patterns of life that we know aren't glorifying to God.

We fall into an old, harmful habit or addiction
    We feel remorse
        We confess our sin
            We experience tremendous guilt
                We try to repent and we say we will do better
                    We then try harder and...
                        We fail again

A cycle of failure seems to repeat itself over and over again. What may be particularly disconcerting is when we have experienced a measure of freedom in a certain area of difficulty, but then a situation may occur that triggers old responses. That was what kept happening to me.

Some of us may have deep pain in our hearts or debilitating fears that appear out of nowhere without a moment's notice. We can't seem to forgive certain people. Our tempers flare-up without warning. We may have a low-grade temperature, as it were, of shame, guilt, or disappointment about ourselves – or what the Bible calls a spirit of heaviness or depression.[3]

Others of us may not be able to let go of a life circumstance – a death, divorce, the loss of health, a job, or a relationship. This keeps us from experiencing the abundant, excessive, over-flowing life Jesus talks about.[4] Our spirits are intact, but our souls are like a city whose walls have broken down[5] and our "enemies" – sinful and rampant thoughts, desires, and habits – have easy access to dominate us no matter how much we want or *will* it to be otherwise.

Where our "Knots" Came From...

The Bible makes it clear we are new creations in Christ,[6] and God sees us clothed in His righteousness.[7] This side of heaven, the Holy Spirit – with our cooperation – is *working out* His righteousness in our daily lives. This is what the religious-sounding word *sanctification* means.[8] Here is a simple way to look at it:

Our Father sees us as an exquisitely beautiful, intricate, and *finished* piece of needlework. This glorious piece of handcraft is so amazing to behold because it is the perfect portrait of the Son of His love. However, the Holy Spirit is busily working on the backside of this masterpiece that we are, where all the knots and loose ends are still hanging out and it just looks like a big old scrambled mess. The Holy Spirit is working on that messy part to cause it to look and become like the portrait itself. Do you get the idea?

> *"For we are God's masterpiece. He has created us*
> *anew in Christ Jesus, so we can do the good things He*
> *planned for us long ago."*
> Ephesians 2:10 NLT

Our *soul* is what needs His healing and His touch, to align with the new creation **we already are**.

Let me ask...has "stuff" happened to you? We all, to some degree, have had *not so good things* happen to us. I'll bet that even as you read this memories might be popping up in your thoughts.

Now, add to the troubling experiences we have had an adversary who hates us passionately. Why does he hate you and me so much? Because we are the image bearers of the Lord Jesus Christ, and the objects of His unfailing love. The enemy despises us because our spirit has been born again and is now filled with the Holy Spirit – God lives within us!

It is in the power of the Holy Spirit that that we do battle against this adversary.[9] We do not wrestle against flesh and blood, but demonic spirits of the enemy. Remember, our spirit is alive and well, however, the devil *still* has access to our soul, that place within us that can be continually *refreshed, restored,* and *renewed* as we daily surrender to Jesus. Nevertheless, the enemy will try anything to keep our soul in a state of confusion and torment – most particularly in our thoughts and emotions. The battle is waged *in* and *for* our soul. As if we weren't already our own worst enemy, now add this guy!

I realize that I am sounding rather light-hearted about all of this, but this is serious truth indeed. Nevertheless, because of our Lord Jesus we have nothing to fear! The enemy is under *His* feet and we have the armor of the Holy Spirit to protect us, and God's Word as the victory sword![10] Still, we need to have real understanding about the spiritual battle that takes place around us every minute of every day.

If you are like me, we would rather have our pastors or spiritual leaders duke it out with the enemy for us, yet we don't have the option to sit on the sidelines. Like it or not, the Bible tells us that we live squarely in the middle of the battle zone here on earth.[11] Lives are at stake – ours *and* the lives of those we love. We have to know a little bit about our adversary and spiritual warfare to start taking back some of the ground we have lost to him in the area of our minds and hearts.

Satan, the devil, Lucifer, the accuser, the tempter, the adversary – whatever Bible name you aptly give him – from all accounts was a key angel that God created to live in the heavenly realms.[12] Beautiful and dazzling, he was corrupted by his pride and rebelled against God by seeking to usurp His sublime and complete supremacy as LORD of all.[13] Because of this, God cast him out of heaven along with lesser angels (now demons, the devil's minions) who had cooperated with Satan's plans.[14]

We learn about these demonic spirits from the Scriptures, especially Jesus' dealings with them as found in the four Gospels. We learn they are without physical bodies and they can take up residence within a person's soul or in an area of their physical being. The original New Testament Greek word for those in the Bible who were tormented by demonic spirits should be translated that these folks were *demonized*. These persons were under the influence and oppression of the enemy and not his possession, as some Bible translations rather inaccurately translate these accounts. However, when great amounts of a human soul is under the influence of a demon(s), it truly seems as if they are possessed in the sense that they are unable to control themselves. A *huge* part of Jesus earthly ministry was the eradicating of these evil spirits from people's lives, and the same is true today.[15]

Here are a *few* examples given in the Gospels and in the Book of Acts of the Lord's Kingdom ministry setting people free from demonic activity in their lives:

- Jesus rebuked a spirit of infirmity from a bent-over woman.[16]
- He also rendered powerless many spirits that He called unclean.[17]
- He rebuked a deaf and dumb spirit.[18]
- He released a boy from a spirit of self-destruction.[19]
- Paul rebuked a spirit of divination (foretelling or being preoccupied with the future) from a servant girl.[20]
- Paul admonished Timothy that he had not received a spirit of fear.[21]

An important truth to always remember is though our adversary, is mighty – ***our God is Almighty!***

"Then the seventy returned with joy, saying, "Lord, even the demons are subject to us in Your name."

And He (Jesus) said to them, "I saw Satan fall like lightning from heaven.""
Luke 10:17-18

Quick recap. We found this serpent of old in the Garden of Eden, **lying** (remember this word for later) to Adam and Eve about God's goodness. He tempted this lovely duo and they too, in their *prideful* thinking that they knew better than God, rebelled and disobeyed His command to *not* eat of the Tree of the Knowledge of Good and Evil. As we have already discussed, not only did Adam's and Eve's fall from the personal, unhindered embrace of the Most Holy Loving God take place, but they handed their God-given dominion to rule this planet into the hands of this evil fallen angel.[22]

The Rescue Mission...

But, Jesus...came.

God became flesh, to rescue us from behind enemy lines. Our belief in the One and Only Savior brought our dead spirits back to life, so that we could have fellowship with our loving Father for eternity.[23] And that is not all Jesus did for us. He came to *untie our knots* (remember the embroidery analogy earlier?) and restore our authority over the devil!

*"He who sins is of the devil, for the devil has sinned from the beginning. For this purpose the Son of God was manifested, that He might **destroy** the works of the devil."*
1 John 3:8-9

Let's take a closer look at the Greek New Testament definition of the word *destroy* from the verse we just read:

Lyo Meaning: To loosen what is bound, to untie. To loose, let go, set free. To dissolve, sever, break, to destroy and demolish, to make void or dissolve.

Make this scripture very personal to you. Jesus came to *destroy, untie*, and *demolish* your hurts, wounds, strongholds, and any lies you may be believing. He also came to do this for the people you love and are in the realm of your influence.

Jesus came so we could be restored as His darling children, the beat of His heart.[24] As His children He has given us His authority to take back the dominion that once was ours, but lost to the devil at Adam's fall.

> *"Behold, I give you the authority to trample on serpents and scorpions, and over all the power of the enemy, and nothing shall by any means hurt you.*
> *Nevertheless do not rejoice in this, that the spirits are subject to you, but rather rejoice because your names are written in heaven."*
> Luke 10:19-20

Somewhere, sometime in the midst of Jesus' rescue mission for my heart and mind, He spoke very clearly to me, *"You believed a lie rather than My truth."* The minute He said this to my heart, I knew it was so. I knew the Word of God, but a lie was quicker, easier, and more effortless to believe. Truth requires *faith* on our part. Lies simply require less effort and less day-in, day-out personal intimacy with God. Think of it this way: my believing a lie was equal to pulling the adversary's veil back over my soul. No more.

It is time for us to make the choice if we really believe the Word of God or not. It is time to start taking Jesus at His Word and engage in the skirmishes and battles the enemy is waging all around us; exercising the power of Jesus Name![25]

The Roaring Lion...

This enemy – who is not only full of darkness – is a *liar*. Jesus, when speaking to the religious leaders who so vehemently opposed Him, said the following:

> *"You are of your father the devil, and the desires of your father you want to do. He was murderer from the beginning, and does not stand in the truth, because* ***there is no truth in him***. *When he speaks a lie, he speaks from his own resources, for* ***he is a liar and the father of it.***"
> John 8:44

Where does the adversary speak his lies? In our minds and through our thoughts.

Often when our souls have been wounded by our past experiences, that same serpent of old – by use of his demons – usually comes to present a lie to us. The enemy does not play fair. He does not abide by the Geneva Convention Treaty for humanitarian treatment during war. He truly is a roaring lion (toothless, yet wily and destructive) seeking whom he may devour as Peter tells us.[26] He is very good at ensnaring us, especially in our early childhood up through puberty when we are most vulnerable, when we would not even begin to know how to resist a lie with truth. Again, is this fair? No! *Remember the devil is pure evil.* When we are at our weakest or are most defenseless, his words *seem to appear as the truth*, confirming what we may have experienced.[27]

- "There you go, you've messed up, AGAIN. You always do or say the wrong thing. Nobody could ever love you."
- "That awful thing happened to you. You are not important. You don't matter. God didn't see what happened."
- "See, you were over-looked…again – you must not be worth someone's time. You do not have value."
- "God's done it again. He has disappointed you. He is not worth trusting."
- "God answered that person's prayer, but not yours. He doesn't really love you."
- "God is sure taking His time about this; maybe you had better take matters into your own hands. He has forgotten you."

The Apostle Paul gives us great warning and advice in one simple phrase:

> *"Be angry, and do not sin": do not let the sun go down on your wrath,*
> ***nor give place to the devil."***
> Eph 4:26-27

What is the original New Testament Greek meaning of this phrase? What does it mean to give the adversary a *place*?

Topos – Meaning: English *"Topography."* A place, portion, ground, or a space marked off. A condition, position or station held by someone, such as in a company or assembly. An opportunity, power or occasion for acting.

Strongholds…

Much like in any war the world has seen where an enemy army has advanced and gained ground, that place has become an enemy *stronghold*. When we give place to the enemy's *lies* for any length of

114

time, it's as if we have made an agreement that these lies *are* true. These lies can become *strongholds* in our soul for him to set up shop and torment us. Most of the time we won't even realize what has happened. He has gained *topography* in our hearts, minds, personality, or intellect, and we cannot free ourselves because these lies now have a *strong hold* on us.[28] These are scratches in the record of our souls we talked about earlier that we just can't seem to get past.

In early childhood we are seldom equipped to recognize the enemy's advances and lies. Many of us were not raised in Christian homes or we grew up in Christian homes that had little knowledge of God's Word in regard to spiritual warfare. God sees everything. He stops *most* of what the enemy throws at us without us even knowing, yet we still live behind enemy lines. In our ignorance and human nature, we often find it is easier to believe the devil's lies rather than have faith in the truth of God's love for us.

What are these lies about? Most generally they fall into one or two categories, or both:

- Lies about you
- Lies about God

We think if we just *try harder* we will have success over these strongholds in our lives. We often experience so much guilt when we fail time after time that we can hardly bear it. Our intentions to break free are good, but we don't have the power to do so without the truth of God's Word and the strength of the Holy Spirit. These strongholds are places where Satan has a territory of our *soul* that has brought *oppression* to our lives. We have made agreements with the enemy because we have believed his lies about ourselves and/or about God, rather than the truth of God's Word. (This is *not* possession by the enemy – he can't touch our spirits, the dwelling place of the Holy Spirit!)

If you think you may have areas of enemy oppression, don't despair. Instead think, "Yes, I do have some knots (don't we all!), but Jesus loves me so much and He is so powerful, these knots are easy for Him to untie. He won't stop until they are completely loosed and I am free!"[29]

When Jesus cried, "It is finished!" on the cross,[30] He completely destroyed the enemy.[31] Victory and freedom are our inheritance in Christ and whom the Son sets free is free indeed![32]

It is amazing how the Scriptures bear this out. From Genesis to Revelation, God's Word repeatedly warns us about the lies of the enemy.[33] As you read the Bible now, you will be amazed at the frequency of this recurring theme.

Pastor Christopher J. Hayward, the President of Cleansing Stream Ministries, succinctly states:

> *"Strongholds are first established in the mind; that is why we are to take every thought captive. Behind a stronghold is also a lie – a place of personal bondage where God's Word has been subjugated to any unscriptural idea or personally confused belief that is held to be true. Behind every lie is a fear, and behind every fear is an idol. Idols are established wherever there exists a failure to trust in the provisions of God that are ours through Jesus Christ."*[34]

As we understand these spiritual principles we will find much of the Old Testament making more sense to us. Think of it. Israel's exodus out of Egypt and entrance to the Promised Land is a type of our own exodus out of the enemy's strongholds in our lives. Our freedom is our Promised Land...our inheritance in Christ. The rebuilding of Jerusalem's walls in the book of Nehemiah is a great study regarding the rebuilding of our broken and battered souls. Instance after instance in the Old Testament are pictures of God's working in our lives.

What God spoke to the Old Testament prophet Hosea applies directly to the devil when He was commanding judgment against the false or lying prophets of Israel:

> *"'Therefore thus says the Lord GOD: "Behold, I am against your magic charms by which **you hunt souls there like birds**. I will tear them from your arms, and let the souls go, the souls you hunt like birds.*
>
> *I will also tear off your **veils** and **deliver My** people out of your hand, and they shall no longer be as prey in your hand. Then you shall know that I am the LORD.*
>
> *"Because with **lies** you have made the heart of the righteous sad, whom I have not made sad; and you have strengthened the hands of the wicked, so that he does not turn from his wicked way to save his life.*
>
> *Therefore you shall no longer envision futility nor practice divination; **for I will deliver My people out of your hand, and you shall know that I am the LORD.**"'"*
> Ezekiel 13:20-23

How do we break the lies of the enemy and gain back the ground he has stolen from us?[35] The answer is...Jesus – the Truth.

> *"Jesus said to him, "I am the way, **the truth**, and the life. No one comes to the Father except through Me."*
> John 14:6

Study Questions...

- Write in your own words what it means to give the devil *a place* in your heart or mind.

- What does it mean for you to have Jesus *destroy, untie,* and *demolish* the *knots* in your life?

- Have you identified possible strongholds in your own life? Share, if you are comfortable.

- Explain why you think it would be important to know and believe God's truth personally?

- If you are sensing renewed hope for your own life or a loved one in regard to freedom from strongholds, describe how you are being encouraged.

[1] Romans 1:16

[2] Roman 7:15

[3] Isaiah 61:3

[4] John 10:10b

[5] Proverbs 25:28

[6] 2 Corinthians 5:17

[7] 2 Corinthians 5:17.

[8] 2 Timothy 2:21

[9] 2 Corinthians 10:3-4, Ephesians 6:10-13

[10] Ephesians 6:10-17

[11] 1 John 5:19

[12] Ezekiel 28:14

[13] Ezekiel 28:15-17

[14] Ezekiel 28:16

[15] Matthew 8:29, Mark 1:34, Luke 4:33-34, 41, Acts 16:17

[16] Luke 13:11

[17] Luke 4:33, 41; Mark 1:34, Mark 3:11

[18] Mark 9:25

[19] Mark 9:17-27

[20] Acts 16:16-18

[21] 2 Timothy 1:7

[22] 1 John 5:19

[23] John 3:16

[24] 1 John 3:1, John 1:12

[25] Ephesians 6:10-18, Mark 16:17-18

[26] 1 Peter 5:8

[27] 2 Corinthians 11:14

[28] 2 Corinthians 10:3-5

[29] 2 Timothy 1:12

[30] John 19:30

[31] Hebrews 2:14

[32] John 8:36

[33] Psalm 15:2, Psalm 63:11, Psalm 64:1-6, Psalm 101:7, 144:11, Jeremiah 13:25, 14:14, 1 John 2:21

[34] Jack W. Hayford, Sr. Editor, *New Spirit Filled Life Bible*, New King James Version (Nashville, TN: Thomas Nelson, Inc., 2002),

Christopher J. Hayward, *Kingdom Dynamics* 2 Corinthians 10:5

[35] Joel 2:25-27

Truly Free

"Then Jesus said to those Jews who believed Him,
"If you abide in My word, you are My disciples indeed.
*"And you shall know the **truth**, and the **truth** shall*
make you free.""
John 8:31-32

It is the Holy Spirit's pleasure to reveal lies we might believe that have allowed the enemy to create strongholds in our minds or emotions. These *knots* may have originated at hurtful times in our past, and they now affect the way we live and may hinder us from fully walking in all God has for us. It is the heart of the gospel of Jesus Christ to untie these knots, heal the broken hearted, and set captives free.[1]

The purpose of this chapter is to encourage you to seek Jesus' words for your life personally so you that can move forward in liberty from strongholds you may be struggling with. I hope to provide some guidance into a time of prayer for you to seek Him for greater freedom in your life.

First and foremost, there is not any *formula* in Christ that can procure freedom! If there was, we wouldn't need to be so utterly reliant upon the Lord, nor be encouraged to cultivate for ourselves the ability to hear His voice so we don't come around this bend of bondage, again.

Everything about God is relational. He will hold our hand and guide us in His truth. He doesn't use formulas; if we make this time of seeking freedom in our thought lives a matter of "to-dos," we will be gravely disappointed. He is all about having a day-in, day-out relationship with us, and He will use this prayer time to draw you closer to Himself. This intimacy with God is why the Christian life is so wonder-filled, fulfilling, and rewarding.

There are several wonderful Bible-based Christian ministries God is using to bring freedom to His people, such as *Cleansing Stream Ministries*, *Freedom in Christ Ministries*, *Theophostic Ministries*, and *Celebrate Recovery*. They may vary in the *minors* of how they minister to those in need, but their *major* tenant for breaking emotional and mental strongholds is the healing power of God's Word.

Finding Freedom Day to Day...

Much of the time, a special specific prayer time for *untying knots* in our souls *is **not*** needed because:

- We are consistently growing and practicing the written truth of God's Word. His Word undermines and destroys the power the enemy's lies. Our Bible should become our BFF![2] The written Word reveals the living Word, the Lord Jesus.[3]

    "In the beginning was the Word, and the Word was with God, and the Word was God.
    He was in the beginning with God. ...

122

And the Word became flesh and dwelt among us, and
we beheld His glory, the glory as of the only begotten of
the Father, full of grace and truth.
John 1:1-2, 14

- We are growing in our flat-out obedience to do God's will. Though we are far from "perfect," our heart's desire to steadfastly choose His way to do life restores territory we may have lost to the enemy. We are living in the way of Truth.[4]

- We are learning to *share* our hang-ups with others. This brings them into the light, because darkness flees in the presence of the Light – the Lord Jesus![5] Many times simple exposure of hidden, nagging thoughts or behaviors is enough to rout the adversary and his stronghold from our lives.

   "This is the message which we have heard from Him
   *and declare to you, that **God is light and in Him is no***
   ***darkness at all**.*
   If we say that we have fellowship with Him, and
   walk in darkness, we lie and do not practice the truth.
   ***But if we walk in the light as He is in the light**, we*
   have fellowship with one another, and the blood of
   Jesus Christ His Son cleanses us from all sin."
   1 John 1:5-7

- We are also learning the importance of praying with other believers when we find we are struggling in any area of our lives. Praying for others also helps us maintain a better perspective of our own lives, and we are finding that the authority we have in the power of Jesus' Name has profound implications for us all.[6]

   "And the prayer of faith will save the sick, and the
   Lord will raise him up. And if he has committed sins,
   he will be forgiven.

123

Confess your trespasses to one another, and pray for one another, that you may be healed. The effective, fervent prayer of a righteous man avails much."
James 5:15-17

Preparation...

If you have an area of your life you are troubled by and you can't seem to find lasting freedom for, it may be time to take it to the Lord, *again*. Here are some additional, important thoughts before you get started:

* First read through this chapter completely to give you an idea of *how* the Lord *may* work. I also encourage you to read the final chapter of this book, which contains several brief testimonies of those who have sought the Lord for their own personal freedom. With this bit of knowledge, you can pray and prepare your heart beforehand.

* Remember: this is not a formula, pixie-dust, or a quick-fix. You are desiring to be free from lies that might be hindering you from moving forward in all that God has for you. This is for the long-haul of your life. Once free, you will need to make the daily choice to walk in God's truth for you. No one can do that for you, but you.

* It is important to keep in mind that our entire journey in Jesus is a road of progressively drawing closer to Him and walking in the Spirit. Our freedom may take place in "layers" or on different levels, much like peeling back old paint to discover the original intent of an artist.

For example, the Lord Jesus helped me break agreements with the enemy regarding a *spirit of pride* that kept me in a cycle of living in a fantasy world. When the final blow was dealt to that stronghold in my thinking that I knew better about my life than God did, I sensed immediate release. Several years later, however, the Holy Spirit was able to go even deeper to show me the original *pride* I had agreed with had its root in a *spirit of shame* that still seemed to oppress me to a small degree. It was a genuine revelation when I hadn't even been seeking the Lord about this area. When *shame* was exposed to me in the quiet of my heart, I sensed an even greater liberty about my life. Jesus' freedom in your life will lead to even greater freedom.

- If you are seeing a counselor (hopefully a Christian one), tell them about the prayer time you would like to have to allow the Holy Spirit to reveal any lies you might be believing. Invite them to partner with you. If they are uncomfortable with the idea of your participating in this type of prayer time, please submit to their leading. You don't want to interfere with how the Lord is already directing your path to wholeness.

- Do **NOT** stop taking any medications you may be taking for any reason! Even as you sense the Lord is healing you in an area in your soul or body, you need to be carefully observed on an on-going basis by a licensed physician before stopping or reducing any medication. It is imperative you heed this warning! I have a dear prayer-warrior, Holy Spirit gifted friend whom the Lord delivered from a lie of shame who still takes her bi-polar medication. No shame there!

- You can certainly meet with the Lord alone, but it is most helpful to have at least one other person you trust, of the same gender, to pray with you.[7] The person should be a solid-in-Christ friend and/or pastor who is knowledgeable of God's Word. I wouldn't go setting up bleachers and inviting the gang over, with chips and dip after. Have your prayer partners read the previous chapter along with this chapter.

Those praying with you should be somewhat quiet, in-prayer observers as the Lord speaks to your heart directly. However, the Holy Spirit may give them insight to help you should you feel stuck or help with the "why or what" questions we will discuss shortly. This is one of the reasons the Holy Spirit dispenses His gifts to the body of Christ – to help us in our time of need.[8] Also, a second or third person may be a great source of encouragement and accountability for continued freedom.

- Be sure to give yourself a good hour or two of uninterrupted time without distraction (no Facebook or Instagram!).

- Remember the Holy Spirit wants your freedom from the lies of the enemy more for you than you do. He is your Helper, your Comforter, your Counselor. He is the One who comes along side of you to help you.[9] He is the Spirit of Truth and He reveals Truth![10] When we invite Him to come into any area of our life…He comes![11]

- If you don't seem to find much help from this prayer time(s), then ask the Lord to direct you to a professional Christian counselor. Don't spend another day living less than all the Lord has for you. God uses professional Christian counselors to His glory!

Time to Untie Some Knots...

We come to the Lord on the basis of His unimaginable love. If you struggle with this truth from the get-go, you have a good place to start looking for lies about your self-worth, and lies about God's immense love for you personally.

Begin by worshipping the One you love so much. Surrender your time to Him and ask Him to speak into areas where He wants to go in your heart and mind. If you have received your spiritual language, this is an appropriate time to use it. Your spirit is in direct communion with God without hindrance from the enemy.[12]

Have you had past exposure to the occult? If you are settled in your heart that you have previously confessed any past practices that may have opened doors for the enemy to oppress you, continue to move forward in your prayer time. If you think there may be past residue in your soul about experiences with openly devilish circumstances such as occult involvement, Ouija boards, horror movies with spiritually dark overtones, books, or whatever you know was dabbling in darkness, cause these occurrences to be fully exposed to the fire of the Holy Spirit's touch. Bring them out into the light through confession and renounce or break any ties that still may linger in your mind and heart.

Is there a family history of a reoccurring stronghold? For example, has there been substance abuse, anger, sexual sins, divorce, abandonment, or violence that has been passed along the generations of your family? There could be any assortment of family "characteristics" that have been manipulated by the enemy. The Bible clearly reveals that the sins of the generations before us can be passed onto us! And, just a surely, the Bible tells us that *we* can be the one who breaks these chains of bondage in the name of Jesus so that our descendants do not have to walk in old family footsteps.[13]

Do you have a presenting issue that seems to be an obstacle to your walk with the Lord or your relationships with others? Simply ask the Lord to bring to your mind a memory of where this may have started. Don't be concerned if it takes a few minutes for a recollection to come. Just wait quietly. You may have a remembrance come to your mind almost immediately, don't dismiss it. You may be tempted to think this past situation cannot be the correct memory that will lead to the root of your area of struggle. However, the Holy Spirit has brought this memory to your thoughts, so please "go" with it. If you are alone, it may be helpful to write in a journal what the Spirit is showing you as you seek Him. If you are with others, just start verbalizing the memory you have.

If the memory is one that is fairly recent, ask the Lord if there is an even earlier occurrence of the same type of situation. Remember, we are most vulnerable to the enemy's lies at an early age. This is kind of like pulling on a vine. We can see the *berry* – the problem – but where the Lord wants to take you is further back to the *root* of the lie.

> *"Examine me, O LORD, and prove me;*
> *Try my mind and my heart."*
> Ps 26:2

> *"Behold, You desire truth in the inward parts,*
> *And in the hidden part You will make me to know wisdom.*
> Ps 51:6

> *"Search me, O God, and know my heart;*
> *Try me, and know my anxieties;*
> *"And see if there is any wicked way in me,*
> *And lead me in the way everlasting."*
> Ps 139:23-24

> *"So He asked his father, "How long has this been happening to him? " And he said, "From childhood."*
> Mark 9:21

It may be only one memory or two or three. From my experience, it doesn't seem to take much and you don't need to relive everything. Don't panic! You will be amazed at how the Holy Spirit takes over as sweetly and gently as a cooing dove, yet, when it is time, He will defeat the enemy with His blazing fire.[14] At some point, and usually it will not take long, you will "hit" a memory that you will want to linger over.

Often the memories the Lord brings to mind may seem fairly innocent and not traumatic. When I came to the Lord regarding my insecurities regarding my appearance that seemed to haunt me, the memory that kept cropping up was a playground experience from the 3rd grade. It wasn't a bad occurrence at all from any stretch of the imagination! However, it summed up what I felt about myself at that time and carried well into my adulthood. I almost dismissed this memory, however the Lord kept bringing it back to me.

One obstacle that may dissuade us from seeking God's freedom in our lives is our thinking we don't have any traumatic experiences to look back on as a source of a stronghold. Still, we have wounds and hurts that have long plagued us. Because these wounds seem innocuous compared to others who have suffered terribly from emotional or physical abuse, we may be tempted to disqualify ourselves from the Holy Spirit's help. However, even off-handed remarks or simple experiences can still be wounding to us. A *hurt hurts*, no matter if was insignificant or gigantic. Some things we just didn't have the ability to "shake off," as it were, when they took place and the enemy took advantage of our vulnerability.

Don't rush this time. Talk about the memory or write out key points. Those who might be with you may ask a few questions for clarification, but otherwise it is best if they just listen – hard for us ladies, I know! Friends will always want to make things better...but it is important that they just listen and don't get in the way!

You may feel as if you are rambling when describing these past recollections – what you felt, what was said, or what was done – that is okay. Just get it all out there. You are exposing wounds to Jesus' healing light.[15]

What, Why, and How...

Now start asking some questions.

- **What** did you feel when the circumstance(s) you are remembering took place?
- **Why** did you feel that way?
- **How** did you react?
- **Why** did you react that way?

You are asking these questions to find the reason a lie was able to be planted in your soul. Don't stop with your first or second response, you want to get to the *root* of the stronghold. Even if you think you have reached the *root*, ask a few more *why did I feel that way* or *how did that make me feel* questions.

I was praying with a woman once who was certain that much of unhappiness was due to a *spirit of rejection*. She recognized that her compulsion to people-please plagued her in almost every situation she found herself in, including ministry. What she realized about herself was true; the root of the lie that enemy plagued her with, however, wasn't rejection – it was the underlying fear of what rejection would reveal: that she was not valuable or she did not have worth. It is important to keep pressing further to the "end of the vine."

Tears may come, and then again, they may not. We are each one-of-a-kind individuals and this time with the Lord will be unique to *you*.

Sometimes people get stuck and honestly don't remember *why* they reacted the way they did or *how* they felt about an incident the Holy Spirit is bringing to the surface. If that is the case, just stop and pray as you feel led. The Holy Spirit may prompt you to pray again for guidance or have you rebuke a *spirit of confusion* in the authority of Jesus' name. Be obedient to do what you are sensing (often, a gentle impression on your heart or mind) even if you are not sure what you are "hearing" is correct. You are not only being set free by the Lord, you are learning to be even more sensitive to what His voice sounds like (gentle, pure, kind, and holy).

If you have another memory from the past, keep *"pulling on its vine."* Keep asking yourself or have others ask the "what-why-how" questions. Don't stop too early. Keep going until you sense you are finished and have reached the final layer of how you actually felt when you had these experiences so long ago. Most of the time we have no clue what we really thought or felt when the incident happened. We may only remember our initial reaction, but have never taken the time to see if there was an underlying factor that triggered our reaction. Don't be surprised to be surprised!

You may reach a point when the Holy Spirit asks you to forgive someone for hurt they inflicted upon you, no matter if it was intentional or not. *This is a necessary step that you cannot skip over.* Even if you have granted forgiveness in the past for the very same event(s) you are remembering now, if the Lord is prompting you to declare your forgiveness again, be sure to follow through. Ask His help for this if you are log-jammed in your heart and are unable to extend forgiveness in your own strength.

Uncovering Lies...

When you sense you have reached the end of the line in response to asking questions about the memory, ask the Lord to show you what the lie is the enemy spoke to you that you have partnered and agreed with.

- Is it a lie about yourself?
- Is it a lie about God?
- Is it both?

First: Is this a lie the enemy has told you about yourself? You may not have had a clue before this prayer time that you even thought this way about yourself! Suddenly you may have understanding regarding some of your behaviors that have puzzled you. Possibly, you may have consciously believed this lie *was the truth* about yourself for a long time, but the Holy Spirit is letting you know it is a *terrible untruth*. When you are ready, give the lie to Jesus – breaking any agreement with it you have made. Use wording that is most meaningful for you in giving up this lie's hold on your life. *Break, renounce, resist, surrender.* The enemy hears your words and the stance you are taking for the Lord's truth regarding who you are and who Jesus is. Render powerless and ineffective every lie and stronghold by name as the Holy Spirit leads you by the authority of the name of Jesus![16]

If this is a lie you have been believing about God, it is the time to own up to it and genuinely *repent* as we have been learning about. You are no longer going to think this way about Him. You are making a 180-degree turn from falsehood to truth. Even the most heinous atrocities which may have been inflicted upon us by others, that made us vulnerable to the lies of Satan about the character and love of God, need to be repented of as *our own failing*.

It may seem unfair we should be held responsible for our choices at vulnerable ages of our early childhood. Nevertheless, as adults, we have carried on in these patterns of incorrect, sinful thinking.

132

Confession and repentance over these erroneous thoughts about the Lord are the beginning of the cleansing process in our lives. Jesus' sacrifice on the cross will become even more significant and meaningful. As Jesus stated, those who are forgiven much, love Him much.[17]

As strongholds of the enemy come to light in the Holy Spirit's presence, you will begin to see clearly where you have been ensnared. Do not worry that you won't get it *right*. The Lord is at work in your midst, and He is gentle as He peels back layers that have covered (remember the veil?) your soul and kept you in a tight grip.

Here is a listing of several lies the devil *may* have used to keep you from Jesus' abundant life:

- Abandonment
- Self Pity
- Rejection
- Deception
- Shame
- Depression
- Confusion
- Witchcraft (Occult practices)
- Fear(s)
- Shame
- Rebellion
- Pride
- Control
- Infirmity (Physical Illness)
- Religion (Legalism/Pseudo Spirituality)
- Lust (All types)
- Gluttony
- Self Protection
- Divination (Preoccupation with the future)
- Perversion
- Anger

"But God has revealed them to us through His Spirit. For the Spirit searches all things, yes, the deep things of God.

For what man knows the things of a man except the spirit of the man which is in him? Even so no one

133

knows the things of God except the Spirit of God.
Now we have received, not the spirit of the world,
but the Spirit who is from God, that we might know the
things that have been freely given to us by God."
1 Cor 2:10-12

After recognizing and renouncing lies you have believed, either about yourself and/or the Lord, you may have a dramatic sense of *release*. Then again, you may feel nothing. We are stepping out in *faith* when we break the stronghold of the enemy's lies in our lives by the power of God's Word and the authority of the Name of Jesus. It is done, regardless of what we feel.

Author and noted speaker, Neil T. Anderson writes:

Freedom from spiritual conflicts and bondage is not a power encounter; it's a truth encounter. Satan is a deceiver and he will work undercover at all costs. The truth of God's Word exposes him and his lie. His demons are like cockroaches that scurry for the shadows when the light comes on. Satan's power is in the lie and when his lie is exposed by the truth, his plans are foiled.[18]

Hearing from the Lord...

Now, for the wonderful part of this healing time. Ask the Lord to speak *truth* to you about yourself and/or about Him. How does He see you? What does He think of you? What does His *truth* have to say to about you, as opposed to the lie you once believed? What is the *truth* about God? What you have been taught and what you know from God's Word will come flooding in. His Word is truth.[19]

Don't rush this time. If you aren't *hearing* anything in your heart or mind, just wait a little longer. As with most aspects of our walk with Jesus, we might sense God is speaking to us, but our first reaction is, "Oh, I'm just making this up." However, you have surrendered this time to the work of the Holy Spirit and He is the One speaking to your heart. *Scripture will back up everything you are sensing He is saying to you.*

As you wait upon the Lord, His words to you may come as a "soft" impression on your mind or in your heart. You may have Bible passages come to your mind or you may hear words gently being spoken personally to your heart. You may see a picture in your thoughts or receive a sense of His love fill your being. Because how He speaks to us individually is so subjective to each of us, it is difficult for me to express exactly how *you* will sense that God is speaking to you.

It is important for you to hear from the Holy Spirit for *yourself* without the help of others. A person may speak an encouraging word to you; however, when the Lord speaks *His Word* into your soul and spirit – it brings healing.[20]

> *"But the wisdom that is from above is first pure, then peaceable, gentle, willing to yield, full of mercy and good fruits, without partiality and without hypocrisy."*
> James 3:17

We have looked at this verse in a previous chapter, but it's good for us to remember what the voice of the Lord sounds like: He brings peace, is gentle, pure and easily understood. His voice is full of mercy, goodness, and is without judgment or hypocrisy. If you hear or see anything that is contrary to God's nature or contradicts the Bible, take time to resist these oppressing thoughts in the powerful name of Jesus.

It is impossible to underestimate the wonder of knowing that Jesus is speaking to your heart. He is speaking truth into lies and situations that may have robbed you of abundant life in the past. Again, ***His word to you will always line up completely with His written word.*** It will be important for you to have Scriptures that correlate with what He tells you. When – not if – testing comes from the enemy, you will need these "anchors" of truth from the Bible. We'll talk a bit more about the power of God's Word in our lives in the next chapter.

The Bible tells us God's judgments are unsearchable, and His ways go beyond our understanding.[21] There is no telling how He may work in each individual's life. When you read the short stories of those who have experienced release from strongholds in their lives, found in the final chapter of this book, you will marvel at their diversity and uniqueness!

Hopefully you are encouraged to press on in the Lord for greater freedom to truly *walk in the Spirit*. Jesus wants you free more than you do – it won't matter methodology or practice – but it must be scripturally based.

If you are fearful about what will replace these old thoughts and behaviors, you are not alone. Most people have no clue what it will feel and look like to walk without hindrance! Be reassured. The Lord Jesus desires to flood every void and overflow every vacancy in your soul with the riches of His grace, truth, and love. It will take time, faith, and cooperation on your part to let go of your wounded past, but the reward is a treasure beyond compare.

> *"But as it is written: "Eye has not seen, nor ear heard, Nor have entered into the heart of man The things which God has prepared for those who love Him.""*

1 Corinthians 2:9

The Lord Jesus has buckets, no – oceans – full of freedom to be found in the healing power of His endless, unfathomable love for you. It is time for us all to run as fast as we can into His refreshing, renewing, and transforming presence.

Are you ready to go?

> *"However, when He, **the Spirit of truth**, has come, **He will guide you into all truth**; for He will not speak on His own authority, but whatever He hears He will speak; and He will tell you things to come.*
> *"He will glorify Me, **for He will take of what is Mine and declare it to you.**"*
> John 16:13-14

Study Questions...

- Explain what it means to have the Lord Jesus desire you to be healed from life's hurts more than you do?

- Which one or two of the paragraphs preparing you for a healing prayer time made an impression on you, and why?

- Do you think asking the *what*, *why*, and *how* questions will be helpful to uncovering possible lies about yourself or God that you may be believing? Explain.

- Do you have any apprehension about pursuing freedom in the manner described in this chapter? Articulate what you are experiencing.

- How important do you think it is to have Scripture support what you sense the Lord would say to you individually? Explain.

[1] Isaiah 61:1-7, Luke 4: 16-21

[2] Best Friend Forever!

[3] John 1:14

[4] 1 John 2:3-5

[5] 1 John 1:5-7

[6] James 5:16

[7] The reason for my "gender suggestion" is that you may be in a somewhat vulnerable place in your emotions during your time of recalling old memories. Again, the enemy does not play fair and I hope you can follow my train of thought without my having to say anything more about it. Of course it is wonderful if your spouse wants to pray with you during this time, and if there is more than one other person, if that third person is of the same gender as you, that is perfectly fine. Give no place to the devil...

[8] 1 Corinthians 12:7-11

[9] John 15:26

[10] John 16:13

[11] Luke 10:9-13

[12] 1 Corinthians 14:2-4. For a more in depth study of the Holy Spirit and His gifts, see *Pneuma Life*, Sue Boldt. Available at www.Amazon.com

[13] Exodus34:7

[14] The dove and fire

[15] Matthew 4:16

[16] Philippians 2:9-11, Luke 10:19, Colossians 2:14-15, Acts 3:6, Acts 16:8

[17] Luke 7:47

[18] Neil T. Anderson, *The Bondage Breaker* (Eugene, OR: Harvest House Publishers, 2000) pg. 23

[19] Psalm 119:160,John 17:17

[20] Psalm 107:20

[21] Romans 11:33

Pest Control

(Establishing Freedom)

"Now to Him who is able to keep you from stumbling, And to present you faultless before the presence of His glory with exceeding joy,"
Jude 24

Everything comes back around to Jesus.
  He is everything.
    He is the bottom line.
      He knows better because He knows it all.
    He is God.

Jesus is the only One who can make sense of life, because He is the One and Only who is life itself.[1] As we have discovered while searching God's Word in previous chapters, our mind and heart are precious prizes to the Lord and He gently calls us to guard them with great diligence. In fact the Bible tells us if we surrender everything in our lives to Him, He will guard our mind and heart for us![2] What a deal! We have also learned that we have a destructive adversary who does not relent in pursuing those he may destroy, yet he is no match for our Lord.

While sitting in an airport just now, I received an email from a dear sister from our church writing to other members of our prayer team. Marjorie had no idea how perfectly her words fit this chapter:

"I was reading in my Bible, "In Him was life, and the life was the light of men."[3]

"The light cannot exist with darkness, so when a believer, out of his free will, chooses the Lord, the Lord heals and gets rid of those dark areas of bondage and lies the enemy has cultivated. It says that the light comes in and the darkness cannot comprehend it. I pictured a lightning bolt lighting up the dark sky. Jesus is so powerful when He invades (in a gentle way) our lives, the enemy and his ways are hit so hard they can't understand the magnitude of what just happened."

As we give the Lord Jesus access to our souls to point His light into our wounded areas and we let Him begin changing the way we view…well…*everything*. He gives us His perspective and we won't want to *lose* all He has done for us.

Maintaining our Liberty...

I found myself being a bit apprehensive the weeks following my marvelous deliverance from the oppression of depression. I was concerned that any misstep on my part might cause me to forfeit my glorious freedom. I had the same misgivings when the yoke of my addiction to food and appearance was no longer a part of my life and again as I was delivered from the final huge stronghold of living in a fantasy world. My *knots* truly were untied, but glancing blows of temptation were still ahead in the coming days, weeks, and years. How was I to maintain my liberty?

All of the disciplines of the Christian faith are essential and necessary. They are our grand inheritance and guidelines to successful living. They develop our authority over the kingdom of darkness.[4] However they are not a list for us to check off everyday. Whenever following Jesus becomes a duty and not the natural overflow of a first-love relationship, He tells us from His word that we have missed Him entirely.[5] We all know too many Christians whose walk with Jesus seems to be more burdensome than most anything the devil could ever throw at them! I was one of those Christians!

Everything God does in our lives is driven by His intense, passionate, and unconditional love for us. Moved by this love, the Lord Jesus implores us to fill the newly set-free areas in our souls with Himself. He further tells us, if we are *not* intentional about securing the now vacant real estate in our hearts and minds, we may be in danger of worse attack and be vulnerable to even greater strongholds![6]

Jesus' words should not make us anxious. They are a healthy reminder of the on-going battle for our souls being waged against us by the adversary. Nevertheless, we have nothing to fear as we remain up-close and personal with the Lord. We have all of the resources we need to defeat the devil and His schemes.[7]

> *"I will not drive them out from before you in one year, lest the land become desolate and the beasts of the field become too numerous for you.*
> *Little by little I will drive them out from before you, until you have increased, and you inherit the land."*
> Ex 23:29-30

These rather obscure verses found in Exodus are similar to those from Deuteronomy that we have read earlier. They are God's words to the nation of Israel as they were about to enter the Promised Land. The word of caution the Lord speaks through Moses states that Israel would rout out their enemies gradually. They could then establish and maintain these territories by inhabiting, building them up, and securely establishing them before moving onto the next conquest. He doesn't want these areas of freedom to fall prey to the enemy (the beasts of the field) again.

This passage is an excellent word for us, too. It encourages us that as we move forward in freedom, little by little, we need to establish His rule in these now vacant places in our soul so we don't give the devil easy access to return. We don't want those *pests* to come back![8] We also learn that God will not move *so* fast that we can't keep up with Him. He is securing our hearts to be tenderly linked to His as greater depths of liberty transform us into the image of His Son.

Peter told us to be sober and vigilant because the adversary doesn't play fair.[9] Paul told us not to be ignorant of the devil's schemes[10] nor be ensnared again by them, even for an hour.[11] It is imperative to shore up, protect, guard, nurture, and build-up these areas of freedom and establish the rule of Jesus where the enemy once governed in our souls. The upside of securing and establishing the Lord's presence in our mind and heart is that we will experience the goal for which this book was written – *refreshing, restoration, and renewal in the presence of the Lord*.

In this and the next chapters, we will explore aspects of our Journey in Jesus that have been personally life transforming and restorative for myself and others. No, not a formula! However, we do need the tools He has provided for us *to*:

- Give us strength to resist daily temptations
- Know what to do when we seem to fall back into an old pit
- Know how to find overwhelming refreshing and satisfaction in God's presence so past snares have no attraction for us and future temptations are empty compared to Him

- Know the living Truth – the Lord Jesus – intimately
- Know the power of the written Word – the ultimate truth
- Have an increasing awareness of the Holy Spirit in our everyday lives to minister freedom and healing to others

The Power of His Word...

There is a high premium on understanding the value of God's written Guidebook, the Bible. In it we find spiritual wealth, practical help for our lives, healing for soul and body, power over our adversary, and personal freedom. Through the Bible we learn about the nature of God, His incredible love for us, the way of salvation, our inheritance in Christ, and how to live the Christian life. The written Word will always lead us to and reveal the Living Word, Jesus.[12] It will be nearly impossible to experience continued clarity and have freedom established in our thoughts without it.

> *"Sanctify them by Your truth. Your word is truth."*
> John 17:17

Yes, God's Word is truth! We need to fill our heart and mind with His written word to discern when the enemy brandishes his lies. This will be especially important for us should we stumble and it appears we have fallen back into an old stronghold. Instead of floundering under the weight of guilt the adversary would try to drown us with, we look to the truth of God's Word which tells us that Jesus paid the debt for our sin and we are completely forgiven and clean.[13]

> *"The steps of a good man are ordered by the LORD,*
> *And He delights in his way.*
> *Though he fall, he shall not be utterly cast down; For the LORD upholds him with His hand."*
> Psalms 37:23-24

This beautiful passage was my "go to" verse when I thought I had lost all of my freedom in a particular area and I was now back at "square one." Although I had stumbled, the Lord was telling me I hadn't fallen all the way down, flat on my face. Instead, He was holding me and I had only scraped my knees up a bit! Ask the Lord to give you "go to" verses that will be personal to you in times of testing.

This may sound harsh, but I won't continue to meet and pray with someone for their continued freedom if I know they aren't reading the Bible and cultivating the practice of hearing of God's voice personally from it. I am not asking for quantity of Scripture or time spent; rather, I am looking for the quality of their reading. In other words, is the person learning to sense when their heart is being touched by the Holy Spirit or that the Lord is speaking to them.[14] All the time and effort to procure breaking of strongholds will be lost if the person doesn't have a personal relationship with God's Word for themselves.

We learn something amazing about the Bible from Paul in his letter to his protégé, Timothy:

> *"All scripture is God-breathed and is useful for teaching, rebuking, correcting and training in righteousness, so that the servant of God may be thoroughly equipped for every good work."*
> 2 Timothy 3:16-17 NIV

Wow! God's Word is literally His breath speaking life into us! It is the Holy Spirit igniting the written Word to pierce into our innermost being (our soul and spirit) to make us more like our Lord Jesus.[15]

Knowing the Bible is a living and God-breathed book changes everything about how we view His Word. Just as our bodies can't live without oxygen, so too our souls and spirits need God's breath to breathe life into us daily.

Besides being our spiritual oxygen, the Bible is also "our daily bread."[16] If we neglect it, our spirits can become anemic. His living Word is spiritual food for our lives and it cuts through all the junk of our soul and gets to the matters of the Spirit. We are then prepared for every situation we might find ourselves in. When we are spiritually anemic, because we are not daily in the Bible, it is much like when we go to the market while our stomachs are hungry: we load up our shopping carts with junk food that normally wouldn't have tempted us.[17] Our life in God's Word is like that, too. When our soul and spirit are filled and saturated with a delicious feast from God's Word, we are less likely to indulge in temptations that ultimately will ensnare and not satisfy us.

If you are fairly new to God's written word, ask the Lord to guide you to specific scriptures for your particular situation. Look up key words to find Bible verses that may be helpful to you, such as *hope, joy, liberty, truth,* etc. You can do this by using the concordance at the back of your Bible (if it has one), a Bible website[18] or a Bible app on your phone. It will also be helpful to ask someone a bit further down the road in their walk with Christ if they may know of any passages that would be helpful for you. It is His Word to you that brings great healing.

> *"He sent His word and healed them,*
> *And delivered them from their destructions."*
> Psalm 107:20

It will also be imperative for you to *continue* in the Scriptures to progressively grow in the truth, learn about God, hear Him speak to you, and to keep walking in and experiencing His freedom. If the Bible is new to you, start with the Gospels Matthew, Mark, Luke or

John. They are wonderful launching pads for discovering who Jesus is. Be sure to use a modern translation of the Bible such as:

- The New King James Version – NKJV
  My personal preference.
- The New International Version – NIV
  I love to compare the wording of the NKJV with the NIV.
- The New Living Translation – NLT
  A paraphrase, but excellent for just starting out!
- The English Standard Version – ESV
  I know several friends and pastors who love this translation.
- The Message – MSG
  A paraphrase with great stylization for today's vernacular.

> *"Then Jesus said to those Jews who believed Him, "**If you abide in My word**, you are My disciples indeed.*
> *And **you shall know the truth**, and the truth shall make you free."*
> John 8:31-32

> *"Therefore if the Son makes you free, you shall be free indeed."*
> John 8:36

Jesus was addressing the religious leaders of His day. Though they were experts and scholars of God's Word, they had missed the heart and power of God. It is possible to know the Bible cerebrally, but if it doesn't progress to our hearts it will be of little value to us except as mere head knowledge. We need to let the Spirit of the living God breathe deep inside of us to reveal truth to us personally. When He uses His Word to speak to us it is life-transforming, encouraging beyond words, and the thrill of our lives.

How I Read...

Because of the depth of the strongholds that encompassed so many years of my life, I literally won't go through a day without exposing my heart and mind to God's Word. For me it has become the air I breathe and the bread of life that satisfies, guides, corrects, and ignites my faith; *especially* during stressful times.

How I currently spend time in God's Word won't necessarily look the same as the reading time and manner best suited for you. Our individual circumstances are unique to each of us; however, I spend a little bit of time in the Bible every morning, with rare exception. Even when my little grandchildren are around who rise in the morning almost as early as I do, I still pick up the Word in the bathroom – need I say more? My morning devotions start my day focused on letting Jesus be the Lord of everything that happens. Reading just a few verses is like receiving a battle plan from the Commander of the Lord's Hosts (Jesus).[19] Often what I read has incredible bearing on what I will experience just a few hours later.

I would term this 'morning time', a devotional-study time. I only read small portions of a book in the Bible that I sense the Lord has directed me to read through. I love to read the notes and explore the cross-references in my Bible and I use several translations to explore the many facets of the English translation from the Hebrew Old Testament and the Greek New Testament. My husband calls me a Bible junkie. This is one addiction I don't mind having!

I also try to follow *a read through the Bible in a year plan*. No guilt allowed! I have only been doing this for a few years and the first time through, I read the entire Bible in ten months. I am currently about three-quarters through now, but I'm heading toward the two-year mark! I use an integrated Old and New Testament plan and you can find a variety of these plans on the internet. Most of these plans are not dated and can be started at any time.[20]

I would only recommend this type of reading-for-distance if the Lord leads you to do it. I struggled with guilt for years when I would start in January and peter-out by the third week into a year-long plan. Now, I read large quantities when I can, but not every day. Reading quickly gives me a wonderful sense of how the Bible all fits together. Plus, I am taking in many passages that may not mean much to me at the time of reading, but come up later when I *do* need them for direction or encouragement or to give to others.

Diving In...

The powerful passage below says it all:

> *"For the word of God is living and powerful, and sharper than any two-edged sword, piercing even to the division of soul and spirit, and of joints and marrow, and is a discerner of the thoughts and intents of the heart.*
> *And there is no creature hidden from His sight, but all things are naked and open to the eyes of Him to whom we must give account."*
> Hebrews 4:12-13

The Word of God is the greatest tool in our lives:

> *"The Bible is the Jesus Follower's Guidebook. No one should leave home without it. It is the Christian's compass, GPS (Guided and Powered by the Spirit) and ultimate resource book. It not only speaks of life, it breathes life into those who read it. It is the believer's*

play book, game plan, battle plan, etiquette book, medicine bag, flashlight, feast basket, and treasure map. It acts as a financial advisor, marriage and family counselor, primary care physician or specialist, and personal assistant. It gives instructions on how to navigate tragedy and triumph; celebrate victory and recover from defeat; and move forward in both loss and success. It can perform heart surgery and heal the mind and body."[21]

While helping a lovely young woman named Carmen walk through some of her issues, it came up in our conversation that she rarely spent time reading God's Word. Though very bright and well educated, the *BIG Black Book* (or in her case, the Bible app on her phone!), was daunting to her, and she felt she couldn't understand it. She was very articulate about the teachings she had heard on Sunday mornings and at a home fellowship group she met with, but she personally was not in the Bible for herself.

Knowing Carmen's story and the absence of God's Word in her daily walk with Jesus caused me grave concern about others in my life and in our church, many of them brand new believers. If they were to recognize the enemy's lies from the living truth of Jesus, plus know the power of the Word for themselves, our church had better start some kind of easy intro to basic Christianity as found in the Scriptures. I wanted them to discover the incomparable thrill of hearing God speak directly to them through His Word. This prompted the writing of the CrossPointe (for gals) and CrossFire (for guys) Discipleship Bible Study Series.

Whether you use the CrossPointe/CrossFire Study Series or any other wonderful study guides available as a help to get started or for deeper study, the simple opening of God's Word for yourself will be the ultimate feast for your mind and heart. There will *never* be a time when your life is not nourished by it. Just as you probably don't remember what you ate for dinner, two weeks ago from last Thursday, you were nourished by that meal. So too, a daily touch from this Living Book will nourish your soul and strengthen your spirit, no matter whether you are aware of receiving something from it or not...believe me! You were nourished!

Knowing the Bible for yourself will build and establish your faith and teach you the truth you will need to know in order to resist and stand firm against the enemy's lies. Don't waste any more time in receiving God's treasure chest of love, hope, peace, encouragement, healing, happiness, and power for your life!

> *"I have not departed from the commandment of His lips; I have treasured the* **words** *of His mouth More than my necessary food."*
> Job 23:12

> *"Then Jesus said to those Jews who believed Him, "If you* **abide in My word**, *you are My disciples indeed.*
> *And you shall know the truth, and the truth shall make you free."*
> John 8:31-32

151

Study Questions…

- Relate what it means for you to establish and maintain freedom in areas of your life that had once been the enemy's strongholds.

- Describe what the Word of God means to you now *or* what you desire it *will* mean for your life.

- Consider your usual schedule for the week. What adjustments do you feel you can make to add at least fifteen minutes in the Bible to your daily routine?

- Share a scripture that is already meaningful to you and why.

- Spiritual oxygen, a satisfying feast, healing for your soul (and body!); which description speaks to your heart most? Explain.

[1] John 3:16 NIV

[2] Philippians 4: 6-7

[3] John 1:4

[4] Ephesians 2:4-7

[5] Matthew 22:29, Matthew 15:18

[6] Matt 12:43-45

[7] 2 Peter 1:4

[8] How ironic that another name for the devil, *Beelzebub*, means "Lord of the flies" in the original Hebrew.

[9] 1 Peter 5:8

[10] 2 Corinthians 2:11

[11] Galatians 2:5

[12] John 1:14

[13] Hebrews 7:27, Hebrews 9:12

[14] Luke 24:32

[15] Hebrews 4:12-13.

[16] Luke 4:4

[17] Thank you Amy Thompson for this illustration!

[18] Try www.blueletterbible.org or www.biblegateway.com

[19] Joshua 5:15

[20] Try: www.blueletterbible.org or www.biblegateway.com

[21] Sue Boldt, *CrossPointe #1 – Building a Firm Foundation* (Charleston, SC: CreateSpace), 2011, Introduction

Refresh!

(Establishing Freedom Continued)

"You will show me the path of life; In Your presence is fullness of joy; At Your right hand are pleasures forevermore. Psalm 16:11

God called King David *a man after His own heart.*[1] No higher praise can be found in all the world. This was not due to David's mighty exploits or that he lived a perfect life (what comfort we can find in these truths!). David was found to be God's darling due to his intense and passionate desire to know the Lord of the Universe intimately. We hear David's longing after his Maker in his beautifully written Psalm:

> **One thing** *I have desired of the LORD,*
> *That will I seek:*
> *That I may dwell in the house of the LORD*
> *All the days of my life,*
> *To behold the beauty of the LORD,*
> *And to inquire in His temple.*
> *For in the time of trouble*
> *He shall hide me in His pavilion;*
> *In the **secret place** of His tabernacle*

He shall hide me;
He shall set me high upon a rock."
Ps 27:4-5

The One Thing...

Lazarus' and Martha's sister, Mary, is applauded by Jesus for her finding the same *one thing* David had discovered. When Jesus visited her family's home, Martha was scurrying about attempting to be Martha Stewart on steroids. Mary, however, sat at Jesus' feet and drank in the deep waters of His words and presence. Martha finally loses it (I've been there, done that!), and impatiently asks Jesus to get Mary to help her. His reply:

> *"And Jesus answered and said to her, "Martha, Martha, you are worried and troubled about many things.*
> *But* ***one thing*** *is needed, and Mary has chosen that good part, which will not be taken away from her."*
> Luke 10:41-42

Mary had discovered the *one thing* David had found; intimacy with the Living Lord.

Refresh, *restore*, and *renew*. These are the words that opened the introduction to our time together. Their reality and experience – not just theory or head knowledge – are what we all long for. Especially in times of stress or anguish. Need I say we probably need refreshment even more when life seems ho-hum, tedious, and mundane? Isn't that when we are most tempted? What is that famous line? "The trouble with daily life, is that it is so daily!"

David and Mary share with us their secret to living life to the full

– the abundant life Jesus promises to His followers. Time alone with Him; sitting at His feet and seeking only His beauty and glory.

I personally prefer to call this time 'the secret place', taken from the New King James Version of the Bible and found in so many places throughout the Scriptures.[2]

> *"He who dwells in the **secret place** of the Most High*
> *Shall abide under the shadow of the Almighty."*
> Ps 91:1

> *"But you, when you pray, go into your room, and*
> *when you have shut your door, pray to your Father who*
> *is in the **secret place**; and your Father who sees in*
> *secret will reward you openly."*
> Matt 6:6

I like to think these passages call this time alone with God as the *secret place* because it is a place only you and He can come to alone, together. He has words meant only for you to hear from His heart.[3] He wants to satisfy and refresh you, providing a bountiful meal for your soul.[4]

> *"Behold, I stand at the door and knock. If anyone*
> *hears My voice and opens the door, I will come in to*
> *him and dine with him, and he with Me."*
> Rev 3:20

Think about it. Just like God's Word, His presence is a feast for your soul and spirit. When you have just enjoyed an awesome meal, savored every bite, loved the company you have shared it with, and you are filled to the brim – you don't need anything else. You are full and satisfied! You are not tempted to indulge in harmful activities – you are simply too saturated with the abundance of contentment and happiness you have just experienced!

How much more our heart and mind is filled to overflowing when they are immersed in the presence of Jesus.[5] The lusts and cravings of this world seem of no value when we invite the Holy Spirit to overflow and overwhelm us.[6] By experiencing *times of refreshing in the presence of the Lord*, old lies that once held us will be less tempting to return to because of the beauty of His presence. Ministry burnout is less likely to take place because we are ministering out of His *fullness* in our lives, rather than ministering on empty fumes. Why settle for a moldy hot dog when you can have Ruth's Chris!

> *"Because of the uniqueness that each of us has in our personal relationship with Jesus, a "quiet time" or "devotional" time will look different from one person to the next. This is not just a time where we come to Him and bring our prayer requests, no, the Lord is calling us to come be with Him for a while, to be refreshed by His presence. He longs to spend time alone with you, and it is our highest privilege to respond to Him. What Adam and Eve lost, we can regain."[7]*

My Experience...

I shared earlier that I spend time in God's Word every morning. This usually lasts fifteen to forty minutes before leaving for work. This is my morning "touch base" time with Jesus. I write in my journal, I worship and pray for immediate concerns. I open my Bible to my current reading place or to another scripture if a different one has come to my mind. I leave those sweet minutes with a settled peace.

Today I was filled with overwhelming joy and a sense of warmth in my being – a true embrace from my Father who loves me! Just like Brother Lawrence who authored the letters in the Christian classic *The Practice of the Presence of God*, I think I am one of God's favorites!

For an uninterrupted extended time to simply wait at the Lord's throne, Saturday mornings work best for me. If possible, I try to carve out time to be in His presence one night a week. Sometimes I may be engaged in a household duty, and I sense the Lord calling me to spend time with Him. Do I always respond? Sadly no. I let the chatter of life drown out His invitation. However, I am learning that the stuff of life will be taken care of, and the reward of being refreshed and renewed is one I don't want to miss.[8]

Once a year I take a personal private retreat to a rustic cabin our family owns. These retreats have never failed to have a profound effect on my life. It was at one of these retreats the Lord Jesus clearly spoke to me out of Isaiah 41:10-13 that an event would be taking place shortly in my life and I was not to be afraid. Two weeks later I was diagnosed with incurable cancer with a seven-month prognosis. The Lord's preparing me for this event was a gift I will never be able to thank Him enough for. The presence of the Holy Spirit and the truth of God's Word from that initial time alone with God has continued to enable me to walk through these past six years in precious peace and exquisite joy unspeakable.[9]

Your Experience...

Your *secret place* will be unique to you and Jesus! For me: I love my front room, on my knees with my Bible, my journal, and a glass of iced tea! I have friends who have found their niche with Jesus in an area of their bedroom. Annie, one of my dear daughters in the faith, shared with me while she and her husband where in the market for a new home, one house in particular was special because she could picture her *secret place* there. That was the home they eventually purchased!

Others that I know have a hard time sitting still, so they have favorite paths they walk, carrying their Bible and pausing to rest when the Spirit speaks to them from the Scriptures. If this time alone with Jesus is new to you, think for a moment right now...where would you like to meet with Him? Make it your *secret place*. He is already there waiting.

How long will this time with the Lord take? Let's put it this way: Give yourself an hour, at least, of uninterrupted time. This may seem impossibly long at first. You may only start out taking a small portion of this time, however, you won't have the pressure of having to be somewhere or having to do something that will put a "ceiling" on this special time with Jesus.

Last week at the CrossPointe Bible Study at my workplace, five of us helped one of our members try to find a time, once a week, to meet with the Lover of her soul. Crystal is a mother of five who works thirty-two hours a week outside of her home. She starts her day at 4:00 in the morning and ends it at 10:00 in the evening. God knows she needed the refreshment! She was tempted to give up her one day-off and take on more work hours. We all encouraged her not to make this decision, but instead trust the Lord for her family's needs as she took an hour or so of her day off to sit at Jesus' feet.[10]

Crystal reported back to us a few weeks after following through with the advice we gave her. She stated she had not felt so rejuvenated in a long time. Her plans for doing laundry and house-cleaning could wait a few more minutes, and she was so much happier when the time came to perform these tasks!

The time is there for you, but as Stacey Eldredge writes in her best-selling book, *Captivating*, you will have to fight for it. It will not come easy, but it is there. Don't let Martha's addiction become yours. You need this time with God for yourself. Your refreshment and restoration will bless everyone around you! Our Lord Jesus, God Himself, who laid aside His Godly prerogatives to walk earth in the flesh, spent time out of His demanding schedule to be with the Father and find refreshment in the Spirit. Could we find a better example to emulate?[11]

Don't be concerned with the amount of time you spend. Yes, try to have at least one hour with the Lord without distraction, but don't get hung-up on counting the minutes. Rather, think of it as if you are meeting a good friend at Starbuck's. You may have all morning or evening; but as you start to converse back and forth, you both seem to know when your time has come to a close. Sometimes you may meet your friend knowing you only have a limited amount of time, however, you are there to enjoy each others company – not do "business." You then proceed with the rest of your day. The exception to this scenario is that you are coming from your *date* with the Lord and you are now filled to overflowing in the love and power of the Holy Spirit! You will soon find yourself losing track of time! The minutes will fly be effortlessly as you cultivate experiencing a taste of eternity.

How many times a week should you go to the *secret place*? This isn't legalism. It is personal heart-to-heart time, so there is no correct answer. Personally, I *need* to have this special time with the Lord Jesus at least once a week! This has been life-saving for me…literally. Since the secret place became a priority for me 10 years ago, I have never been busier in ministry in my entire life, yet without any sense of burnout.

Remember this is not a duty. You are cultivating your in-love relationship with the Lord. This is different from the times you pray, bringing Him your laundry-list of requests or time spent learning more of God's Word. In these moments your heart is seeking His heart. What romance was ever driven by obligation?

I find it helpful to have my Bible and a journal handy to record what the Lord might share with me.

> *"Thus speaks the LORD God of Israel, saying: 'Write*
> *in a book for yourself all the words that I have spoken*
> *to you."*
> Jeremiah 30:2

The Holy Spirit may speak directly to my heart through an impression of what He is saying, a picture I might see in my mind or by a scripture. One Bible passage may lead to another. Everything I sense He is sharing with me will be verified by the Bible. Though I am coming just to be with Him, He may eventually lead me in prayer for others and give me specific instruction on how pray effectively or battle spiritually. This time is His, and He will lead me (and you) through it.

In John's Gospel we learn it is the Holy Spirit who reveals Jesus to us and guides us into all **truth**.[12] As a Christian you have the Holy Spirit residing in you *fully* and *completely*, as we have studied earlier. Nevertheless, if you are not yet sure that you have experienced the overflow or baptism in the Holy Spirit that Jesus promised,[13] simply ask the Lord to give you this precious gift now.[14] The attending gifts of the Spirit are yours.[15] and He will aid you in revealing and nurturing what He has deposited in you.[16]

The Holy Spirit's gift of spiritual language will be of great benefit during your special time alone with the Lord. It is the Holy Spirit igniting our born-again spirits with a language directly from our spirit to the throne of God. By this new and unknown language, we are built-up and encouraged in our faith. Often it is like a *roto-rooter* to our clogged lives when we are confused or weary. This language breaks through barriers of our understanding, bringing us into God's presence.[17] There are many wonderful study books for you to learn more about the power and gifts of the Holy Spirit in the believer's life.[18] And, of course…nothing beats reading the New Testament for an up close and personal glimpse of His practical working, splendor and greatness.[19]

If spending time cultivating intimacy with the Lord is new to you, your first time may seem awkward. You may not sense or *hear* anything. It is difficult for us to say, "Hush," to our busy lifestyles. Nevertheless: As you persist in making the *secret place* a priority, you will find genuine refreshment and restoration. You will not want to go back to living life without this precious and powerful time with God. He desires these moments with you more than you do! You were created for this and for Him. You will receive what you need from Him directly, and no work of darkness, any person or difficult circumstance can take that away from you.

Let's press forward!

> *"How precious is Your lovingkindness, O God! Therefore the children of men put their trust under the shadow of Your wings.*
>
> *They are abundantly satisfied with the fullness of Your house, And You give them drink from the river of Your pleasures.*
>
> *For with You is the fountain of life; In Your light we see light."*
> Psalms 36:7-9

Study Questions...

- Explain why you think establishing newly found areas of freedom is important.

- Share your current relationship with God's written Word, the Bible. No guilt allowed!

- Think about your day. When are you at your best *daily* to crack open God's Word and let Him speak directly to your heart? (Act upon what you write...you won't regret it!)

- Relate how knowing God intimately is important, and what it might mean for you. Share any hopes or fears.

- Now, look at your week. Where could you carve out and fight for an uninterrupted hour to have a "secret place" time with the Lord Jesus?

---

[1] Acts 13:22

[2] Psalm 27:5, Psalm 31:20, Matthew 6:18

[3] Psalm 25:14

[4] Psalm 23:5

[5] Psalm 16:11, Psalm 36:8, Isaiah 55:2, Jeremiah 31:14

[6] Romans 5:5

[7] Sue Boldt, *CrossPointe #1 – Building a Firm Foundation* (Charleston, SC: CreateSpace), 2011, page 56

[8] Matthew 6:33

[9] Ephesians 3:20-21

[10] Matthew 6:33

[11] Luke 5:16

[12] John 16:13-15

[13] Luke 24:49, Acts 1:8, Acts 10:44-48, Acts 19:1-7

[14] Luke 11:9-13

[15] 1 Corinthians 12:6-11

[16] 1 Corinthians 2:9-12

[17] 1 Corinthians 14:2-4, 14-15

[18] *Pneuma Life*, Sue Boldt (found on Amazon.com or by contacting) me at susanboldt@gmail.com

[19] John 16, the Book of Acts, 1 Corinthians 12-14, Ephesians

Keeping the Veil Lifted

(Establishing Freedom Continued)

"...that you may walk worthy of the Lord, fully pleasing Him, being fruitful in every good work and increasing in the knowledge of God."
Colossians 1:10

As we have allowed the Holy Spirit to bring to light hidden lies of darkness in our lives, we need continual encouragement to keep our hearts and minds established in the freedom we are experiencing.

"This is the message which we have heard from Him and declare to you, that God is light and in Him is no darkness at all.

If we say that we have fellowship with Him, and walk in darkness, we lie and do not practice the truth.

But if we walk in the light as He is in the light, we have fellowship with one another, and the blood of Jesus Christ His Son cleanses us from all sin."
1 John 1:5-7

Oh no! You mean we need to be in a local church? Possibly we have been deeply hurt by someone in a church setting or we have been wounded by the church-at-large. As it has been coined, "Church would be great if it weren't for the people!" Nevertheless, we need our church family if we are to continue on our path of ever expanding freedom.

The church of Jesus Christ *is* people – not a building we go to. *We* are the body of Christ as Paul clearly relates to us in 1 Corinthians 12 and Ephesians 4.

> *"from whom the whole body, joined and knit together by what every joint supplies, according to the effective working by which every part does its share, causes growth of the body for the edifying of itself in love."*
> Ephesians 4:16

Each of us needs the Lord to guide us to a local church body. A human body is considered handicapped if a limb or appendage is missing. How much more the Body of Christ needs every member functioning in wholeness. He wants us to be *knit together* with one another. Knit just like a sweater, with no gaping holes in it because you are not there! *You are needed*! We need others and they need us if we are to become more like Christ, reach a lost world, find healing and encouragement, and be edified in love. Even if Georgina in the third row acts so tacky during pot-lucks!

> *"As iron sharpens iron, So a man sharpens the countenance of his friend."*
> Proverbs 27:17

No we may not always agree with one other. Nevertheless, the Lord has *chosen* to use our experience of living life together with other believers, through thick-and-thin, to refine and purify us. Church is where we learn to serve, give and receive, and helps us discover and fulfill God's personal destiny for our lives. And…it is one of the main tools He uses to transform us into the image of the

Lord Jesus.[1]

Look for a church teaching sound Bible doctrine (again, another reason to know the Word of God for yourself),[2] and has a lead or senior pastor who genuinely cares for their flock.[3] Worship should have a high priority in any church you might attend. The style of worship, traditional or contemporary, is unimportant; however, you will want to look for worship that escorts you into the greatness of God's presence.[4]

Our need for accountability and encouragement is huge as we walk out of former lies from the adversary that once captured regions of our soul.

> *"Let us think of ways to motivate one another to acts of love and good works.*
> *And let us not neglect our meeting together, as some people do, but encourage one another, especially now that the day of his return is drawing near."*
> Hebrews 10:24-25 NLT

Find an accountability partner from your congregation that you trust has an ever deepening walk with the Lord, is knowledgeable of the Bible, and has your best interests at heart. This should be someone who is willing to speak God's truth in love to you when you need it. It should not be a person who will let you "off the hook" should you stumble, but gently get you back on the track of God's truth.[5]

If this individual you hope to be accountable to was not a part of your prayer time to be released from the enemy's hold, explain what has taken place for you and inquire if they would carefully consider being someone you can contact for prayer should you have need. You may want to invite this person to frequently "check in" on how you are doing. It can be scary business for us to become vulnerable to another's insight and help, nevertheless, it is necessary for our continued walk in the liberty of the Holy Spirit.[6]

We each have much to offer the Body of Christ. Yes, you do, too! I can hear the doubts in your mind already – resist them! As we continue to press forward for wholeness in our lives, we will have much to give away to others. We should have no fear of not being far along enough on our pathway of freedom to start discipling others in Christ. Many times, our wholeness hinges on our *giving away* what we are experiencing and learning from God's Word and from the practical application of His Word in our lives.

> *We need to be in intentional-discipleship-mode and this is for our growth in God, as well. Knowing that someone is not only being taught by us, but that they are observing our lives, keeps us humble before the Lord to stay on His course for us. Even sharing about wrong turns we have made can spare someone else from making the same detour. We need to be looking over our shoulders and purposely find those with whom we can invest our lives in. Jesus didn't call us to become reservoirs of knowledge and experience, but to be rivers that His Spirit can flow out of into others.*

> *Discipleship is a HUGE reward and blessing to our lives. Don't let others who are moving forward on the Lord's course of investing their lives into others have all the fun!*[7]

Church is where we learn about the magnificence of our God, His grace, healing, and power. We learn that as we allow Him to pour Himself into our lives, investing time with other believers will also encourage us to pour what we have received into everyone around us. Keep your heart and mind from a consumer mentality. Church isn't only about receiving more for *your* spiritual walk, but it is the launching pad for *giving ourselves away*.

Don't Pull the Veil Back On...

Finally, to maintain our freedom the Holy Spirit has secured for us, we must return to what we learned in the first chapter. We need to intentionally *guard our hearts and minds*.

> *"Therefore bear fruits worthy of repentance,"*
> Matthew 3:8

We have studied that true repentance is a change in our thinking from our thoughts to God's thoughts. When John the Baptist tells us to *bear fruits worthy of repentance,* he is calling us to align our actions with our new way of thinking. True repentance will be seen outwardly in how we conduct our lives.

> *"Therefore **gird up the loins of your mind**, be sober, and rest your hope fully upon the grace that is to be brought to you at the revelation of Jesus Christ;*
> *as obedient children, not conforming yourselves to the former lusts, as in your ignorance;*
> *but as He who called you is holy, you also be holy in all your conduct,*
> *because it is written, "Be holy, for I am holy."*
> 1 Peter 1:13-16

I believe that Jesus had completely broken the stronghold of the daydream world in which I used to live in much earlier than I had realized. My problem was not only that I believed that every temptation to daydream was a sinful act on my part, but I would *sabotage* my freedom by continuing to indulge in reading materials,

169

television, and movies that fed the lying spirit who had ensnared me. I kept pulling the enemy's veil back over my heart and mind. This was much like an alcoholic who leaves an Alcoholics Anonymous meeting and heads to the nearest bar to see if he can handle one drink. I needed to give the Holy Spirit a broad place of grace to set up shop in the once-wounded areas of my soul, without the distraction of purposely exposing myself to temptations I was vulnerable to.

Yes, much of what the Holy Spirit initiates on our behalf is instantaneous, never to return, absolute freedom. More often, He is helping us secure ground by taking the time to sow seed, establish a settlement, and live in the land of freedom as we read at the outset of this chapter. Hard won freedom by the Holy Spirit and our cooperation is not something we will easily want to forfeit!

We have learned from God's Word that we now live in God's kingdom of beyond-reason love. He has lifted the dark and evil veil of the enemy from over our minds. Yet how easily we can pull that veil back over ourselves if we are not careful!

> *I will sing of mercy and justice;*
> *To You, O LORD, I will sing praises.*
> *I will behave wisely in a perfect way.*
> *Oh, when will You come to me?*
> *I will walk within my house with a perfect heart.*
> *I will set nothing wicked before my eyes;*
> *I hate the work of those who fall away;*
> *It shall not cling to me.*
> *A perverse heart shall depart from me;*
> *I will not know wickedness.*
> Psalm 101:1-4

Here, we again find King David giving us direction. He was careful to guard truth and purity in the inward man by what he allowed himself to be exposed to. We also see that David found himself in deep trouble when he became lax in guarding his life.[8]

This is not legalism. This is for our freedom![9] Paul tells us: all things that are not sinful in nature are available to us, but *not all* things are helpful or edifying.[10]

When I first began to walk in liberty in regard to my appearance, I found I was vulnerable to set-backs when I indulged in glossy fashion magazines. I was tempted to return to old lies about my worth based on comparing myself with those in the beautiful photos. Now, I am able to enjoy these periodicals with no problem. The irony is that I'm just not interested in them anymore! In another instance, I have a friend who was tempted to return to a *spirit of poverty* when she browsed through reading material featuring nice homes, architecture, and interior design. She would be enticed to feel that she didn't measure up. Pay attention to areas of vulnerability in your own soul and protect and reinforce those places of potential weakness.

> *"Therefore strengthen the hands which hang down,*
> *and the feeble knees,*
> *   and make straight paths for your feet, so that what is*
> *lame may not be dislocated, but rather be healed."*
> Hebrews 12:12-13

Sometimes, guarding our freedom means we will need to decrease exposure to certain relationships that have been toxic to us in the past. Distancing ourselves completely from company that may entice us to be ensnared in old familiar lies. Guarding our hearts and minds means knowing how to establish boundaries with folks who are not encouraging to our health and well-being.

We also may discover that we need to drastically change how we once spent our free time. For example, instead of sitting in front of our computer or tablet, looking for an escape to medicate our pain as we did in the past, we may need to gravitate toward different activities. Because Jesus has healed or is in the process of healing our past wounds that once robbed us of so much life in Him, we may find that we have more free time! Now, when we have moments of relaxation, instead of engaging in old activities that might tempt us to go backwards, instead, let's move forward in our healing. What makes *you* feel happy? Encouraging fellowship with a friend at a local coffee shop? Being outside taking a walk or heading to the beach (my personal favorite!)? What activities do *you* delight in that do not expose you to potential downfall?

Do not exchange one unhealthy addiction for another! Before our lies were revealed and broken, we may not have been able to *choose* what the Lord would have us do. But now that we are free from Satan's grip in these areas, we *do* have the ability to make the *right choice*. Jesus has given us a *sound mind*.[11]

> *"For God has not given us a spirit of fear, but of power and of love and of **a sound mind**."*
> 2 Timothy 1:7

Sophronismos Greek: A combination of *sos*, "safe," and *phren*, "the mind"; hence, safe-thinking. The word denotes good judgment, disciplined thought patterns, and the ability to understand and make right decisions. It includes the qualities of self-control and self-discipline.[12]

Being careful does not mean we are not truly free. Rather, we are taking a stance to guard that freedom. We are to walk our daily lives out carefully.[13] As the Bible tells us, why give place to a potential struggle in the first place?[14]

Ask the Lord to specifically reveal to you where you might have areas of life that seem to sabotage your freedom. Just as the Holy Spirit was faithful to take you to the deep recesses of your soul to find lies that held you, He will now guide you to what will build-up and establish God's territory in your life.

Conclusion...

> "I say then: Walk in the Spirit, and you shall not fulfill the lust of the flesh."
> Galatians 5:16

Forever and always God is on our side. He wants us to live extremely abundant, excessive, overflowing, continually refreshed lives in the power of the Holy Spirit. What could be more wonder-filled than that? Oh my! Just read the book of Acts if you need convincing! No matter what we face, His heart longs for us to realize that we are more than conquerors through Him who loves us.[15]

The simple exchange of our will for God's will and our thoughts for His thoughts will enable the Holy Spirit to heal, restore, and transform our soul. I pray that you have gained a few more tools to destroy the enemy's strategies towards you, and that the Lord's intentional, breathtaking work in your life will be rich and immense.

As we journey with Jesus, one step at a time, into greater depths of health for our heart and mind, we will discover that His *refreshing*, *restoration*, and *renewal* are contagious! Others will begin to see His amazing grace in us and long to dance in His refreshing waters for themselves.[16] Can you think of anything better?

> "For I know the thoughts that I think toward you, says the LORD, thoughts of peace and not of evil, to give you a future and a hope."
> Jeremiah 29:11

Study Questions...

- After reading this chapter has your view changed regarding the importance of belonging to a local church? Explain.

- Name some of the important aspects of church life that you think will help you to maintain your freedom in the Lord Jesus.

- Relate any past practices that have caused you to stumble or perpetuate the enemy's strongholds in your life that Jesus is now urging you to keep your distance from.

- Think and pray about some new activities that will help keep your heart and mind established in your hard-won freedom. List these new avenues as they come to your mind.

- What is your biggest take-away from reading this book, and why is that so?

[1] John 13:34

[2] 2 Timothy 3:15-17

[3] 1 Peter 5:2-3

[4] John 4:23-24

[5] Ephesians 4:15

[6] 1 Thessalonians 5:11

[7] Sue Boldt, *Staying On Course, CrossPointe #3* (Charleston, SC: Createspace, 2012), pg. 73

[8] 2 Samuel 11:1

[9] Psalm 18:21, Psalm 119:37, Romans 12:9

[10] 1 Corinthians 10:23

[11] 2 Timothy 1:7

[12] The New Spirit Filled Life Bible, note: 2 Timothy 1:7

[13] Ephesians 5:15

[14] 1 Corinthians 9:24-27, Ephesians 4:37

[15] Romans 8:37

[16] Revelation 21:6

Stories
of
Freedom

*"And they overcame him by the blood of the Lamb
and by the **word of their testimony**, and they did not
love their lives to the death."*
Revelation 12:11

The power of our own personal testimony cannot ever be underestimated. Hearing the stories of those who have experienced *refreshing*, *restoration*, and *renewal* directly from the Lord Jesus will encourage and build your faith for *your* own life. As you daily follow Jesus and surrender to His ultimate, amazing life journey, you will continually find every day is an adventure and that Jesus is more than enough to meet your every need and desire. Please be encouraged as you read, and yes, each person's name has been changed for these accounts.

Carmen is a dear young woman I work with. One day the Lord sweetly and gently revealed lies she believed about herself and God while we were standing at the copy machine! This proves that God can work anywhere, at anytime, and that He *wants* to! Carmen and I had been talking off and on for a few months at our worksite about issues that had erupted in her life that almost caused her to lose her marriage. This particular day, the Holy Spirit peeled back some final layers of ground taken by the enemy.

Deep issues of abandonment by her biological father and sexual abuse at the hands of her step-father during childhood had caused Carmen to scramble to protect and provide for herself. She had an uncontrollable need to please others (to her own harm) to ensure she would never be alone. This need escalated in the face of a marriage that wasn't all she had hoped for. She was held captive to the desire to be pursued by a man to satisfy deep longings of male affection that were never afforded her by her father or step-father. The very ones who should have protected and nurtured her (including her mother) had completely failed her.

The Lord did a marvelous work in front of that Lexmark machine as He went deep into her heart and old wounds were healed. The lie she believed centered around a fear that Jesus would abandon her because she was unworthy of anyone's love, especially His. In her own words: she believed she was *expendable*. Not wanted or loved. Carmen also believed a lie that she had to provide for herself because the Lord would not take care of her or love her unconditionally. No one else ever had. What a heavy burden to bear.

Tears of freedom flowed. The Lord spoke to her of His tremendous love and care for her. Within weeks she experienced an overflow of the Holy Spirit, causing her to experience the Lord in a way she never had before. Carmen began to move in the gifts of the Spirit and share boldly of her new found freedom. Because of the profound change in her life, her friends and relatives began inquiring how they might find such peace and happiness. Carmen has led several of these loved ones to the Lord to begin their own journeys in Jesus.

Prior to Carmen's breakthrough from the lies of the enemy, her attempts to read God's Word left her confused and frustrated. At the point of her release from the strongholds that had held her, a new-found hunger for the Bible emerged in her heart, causing her to become an ardent student of God's Word. Truly her *veil* has been lifted!

Several months after the copier event, while we were both participating in a work-site CrossPointe Discipleship Bible Study, I casually mentioned a verse which she immediately looked up in her favored New Living Translation.

"Even if my father and mother abandon me,
the LORD will hold me close."
Psalm 27:10 NLT

The perfect wording from this verse spoke to her prior experiences and has become one of her "life verses." These words are a refuge of encouragement and wholeness to her and is only one of many Scriptures the Lord has used to bring Carmen happiness and deep contentment.

Now almost three years later, her marriage is still a work in progress; however, her husband recently acknowledged how much Carmen has changed! He is now making slow movements toward faith, having previously renounced any need for God.

Wherever she is, a huge smile lights up Carmen's face whenever she mentions or shares with anyone who will listen about the lavish love God has for her. Not just in the midst of her current circumstances, but also in the face of the parental abuse and abandonment from her childhood. She now effectively leads a home Bible Study group and she is a fountain of encouragement to everyone, both believer and non-believer alike. Her life demonstrates the power of God's Word to annihilate our foe.

Mike had noticed a cyclical pattern of over-achievement and depression he felt unable to break free from. He also had struggles with same-sex attractions and he sensed all three of these strongholds were connected in some way. After some sessions of prayer and counseling with Randy, the Holy Spirit uncovered a *spirit of control* dominating Mike's life. The original issues Mike sought counsel for were only the symptoms of a deeper root.

In Mike's own words:

I felt like I was trying to untangle ropes where I was only really moving the knots around. I believed God loved me, but something was preventing me from fully receiving it. When Randy challenged me to identify the lie I believed about God that was allowing for control to have a grip in my life, I realized the lie was "God loves you... conditionally." I knew theologically that I didn't earn God's love, but I was terrified of losing it by not being good enough.

This lie led me to make destructive vows in my life: I vowed to be perfect and to be unique so that I would continue to be worthy of God's love. Homosexuality for me was not an issue itself, but just the fruit of these deeper problems. The lie was blocking me from being able to fully receive love from my peers, from my parents, and from God. When I went through puberty I was desperate for love, but unable to consciously recognize it. With my vow to be unique and special to get attention and my emotional rejection by my dad for his failures, homosexuality appeared to meet my needs.

In prayer I renounced the destructive vows and I forgave my father, but I still needed to know where the lie about God's love being conditional had originated in my life to be able to fully destroy it.

Randy said most things happen between the ages of five and seven, so I asked God to show me. I finally came to a memory of hiding from my parents when they wanted to take a family picture. When I heard them discuss calling the police because I was missing, I knew the gig was up and I had to reveal myself and face the consequences.

I felt like God prompted me to look into this memory, but I could not remember why I was hiding in the first place. During prayer, God spoke to me, "Your sister." I went to my parent's house to do research and found the family photo from that day. My extended

179

relatives were there and so was my newborn baby sister! I recalled I was four and a half when my sister was born and on this day I was no longer the center of attention. Wounded and upset, I chose to hide from everyone.

God revealed to me the clue to unlock the memory had been blocked. If I could lose my status with my family, be replaced as the center of attention, then I needed to take control to make sure that never happened again. Most importantly, I had to be careful I never lost favor with God. Knowing where the lie began, Randy and I spoke truth into the deepest part of my life.

Freely receiving the fullness of God's love for me is the only thing that allows me to walk free of depression, free of uncontrollable homosexual urges, and free of perfectionism. Now that the lie is broken at the root, I am on my journey of discovering the full depth of God's love for me.

Tom was a man in much need of deliverance from pornography and drug use. When waiting on the Holy Spirit with Randy, Tom recalled a one-time childhood trauma of sexual abuse that took place at an extended family reunion. The depth of his agony through all of the years since that incident poured forth in their prayer time together.

What the Holy Spirit impressed upon Tom, however, was far different than what he had expected. Tom realized he had agreed with a lie leading him to believe he should be *allowed* or he was *deserving* to indulge or medicate his emotional pain by the use of sexual images and substance abuse because of what had happened to him.

When Tom realized his partnership with a *spirit of self pity*, he was able to recognize it, break his agreement with it, renounce it, and ask God's forgiveness. He next experienced the loving words of Jesus in a profound way. Thoroughly washing away his guilt and shame. God's healing words have brought transformation to his life by giving

Tom the ability to recognize and overcome old temptations and no longer have the need salve his wounds with sinful acts.

Kimmie came to me for prayer regarding the voices she was hearing in her mind which were beginning to frighten her. I had known her for a few years and I always wondered why it was hard to pin-her-down regarding her walk with Christ. She loved the Lord, but many times she seemed like a frantic butterfly flitting from one idea to the next.

With Kimmie's permission, I asked another trusted sister in Christ, Kareen, who is knowledgeable in the Word of God and comfortable in the gifts of the Holy Spirit to pray with Kimmie and I (I rarely pray with someone alone). Before coming together in prayer for Kimmic, Kareen and I set aside time to fast and pray. Abstaining from a few meals often allows greater focus on prayer and the diminishment of the enemy's works in certain occasions.[1] When I sensed the enemy had a deeper grip on Kimmie's life than I had first realized, I called in Randy to pray with us.

Kimmie's memories were long and rambling. The Holy Spirit was pulling on *vines* in her soul that had been growing for years. He wanted her to get to the root of her strongholds. As childhood events came to the surface, she started to receive true insight as to what had occurred to her. Words of knowledge and the spiritual gift of discernment came forth from those of us praying for Kimmie as the Lord gently moved in our midst.

At one point when asked how she felt during a particular childhood event, she said she felt *void* of emotion regarding it. I was reminded how the word *void* is used in Genesis 1 regarding the empty world before creation. Part of the definition of the Hebrew word that is translated *void* in our English Bibles is to be *worthless*. Kimmie at first was unable to relate to a sense of worthlessness and even said so. She was a confident individual in her eyes and the eyes of others. Nevertheless, as she pondered the possibility of worthlessness in her life, the floodgates of her soul poured open as she couldn't stop her tears from flowing. She had been unemotional throughout the whole prayer time until this moment. For the first time ever, in many, long years, Kimmie realized that she had been living her life based on a lie that she was *worthless*. When the enemy's *veil* was lifted from her heart and mind, that lie was broken!

In her own words (names changed) Kimmie also remembers this happening during our prayer time with her:

Randy asked me if the name, "Oliver," had any meaning for me. When he said that name, I immediately thought of my college roommate, Sandy Oliver. This was a personal confirmation the Holy Spirit had showed up for me. I hadn't wanted to share any of this because I was kind of embarrassed and my childhood wounds were enough for me to share during that night of prayer.

When I was in my third year of college I got pregnant and, because I had a "future" ahead of me, I considered an abortion. Sandy was so impartial to the idea, but she became pregnant too. We talked about how we could be moms together and support each other. Well, the end result was we both had abortions. She had to go to counseling to talk about the guilt, but I just pretended it never happened...until the night Randy asked me if the name Oliver meant anything to me. In my talks with Sandy, we said we would name our kids after each other. I believe my aborted child's name is Oliver and is in heaven.

A few nights after the night with you, Kareen, and Randy, I did tell God I knew what He meant by that name Randy had for me and I repented. What a stronghold that was in my life that I never knew about! After I repented, I found myself immediately more gentle with my own kids and rebuking any type of seeds that may have been planted by Satan through my abortion. God is so gracious!

The prayer time we had with Kimmie was the beginning of the end of major strongholds in her life. Idol worship in the form of fear and unbelief, as well as, a generational family practice of idolatry, were exposed in the light of Jesus. As Kimmie saw for the first time how her belief system about God was incorrect, she renounced the darkness she had allowed and the lineage of strongholds passed down to her through her family.

Kimmie is now one of our church's prayer counselors and she is a mighty woman of God's Word: both teaching and discipling others. She is a huge asset to the Body of Christ and to me, personally.

Cathy was a visitor to our church, but in desperate need of help for her marriage. Since her husband was unwilling to receive counsel, I agreed to meet with her to ask the Lord's help for her own issues (which is usually the basis for marital counseling in the first place!).

When Cathy met with our prayer team, she was convinced the Lord was going to focus on one particular aspect of her life. We didn't know her, and we had no preconceived idea of how the Lord might lead us as we ministered to her. The Holy Spirit began to bring up situations and issues surrounding her biological father. Cathy had been so sure these hurts had been dealt with long ago. The Lord knew better, because these were the memories He zeroed in on.

Lies of loss and having to secure her own future were a part of what came forth. Both how she related to her husband and to the Lord were impaired by the toxic and unhealthy relationship she had with her barely-seen birth father, and *not* with her step-father, as she had once thought.

Cathy was brought to a place of forgiveness for many who had hurt and disappointed her in her young life. Because she had projected onto the Lord characteristics of abandonment and poverty which her birth father had exemplified, she repented of these lies and asked His forgiveness. In doing this, she discovered newly found faith. In the past, she had always struggled to really believe that Jesus would or could take care of her problems, most particularly, her finances. A new excitement about following Jesus was reignited for Cathy.

Lisa experienced sexual abuse from her step-father from eight years of age until her early twenties. She was soon to be married, and she was aware that she still needed greater freedom. She did not want to take any remnants of old baggage from her past into her new life with a godly man she adored.

Though in her mid-twenties, Lisa had walked with Jesus in steadfast obedience for a few years. Her self-worth was being made whole in her identity in Christ. However, the *root* of a lie that remained in her heart was the fear that God would not take care of her. Oppressive spirits of the enemy compelled her to feel that she needed to manipulate and control people and situations to her advantage.

After meeting with our prayer team a few times, real victory was secured. Lisa then participated in a Christian sexual-abuse support-group, which further cemented God's healing in her life. Randy and I together had the joy and privilege of marrying Lisa and her husband in a joyous ceremony! She is now completing her medical residency program, and the happy couple hopes to serve the Lord in long-term missions in Tonga.

Shelly came to me because her marriage was in shambles. She had little-to-no control over her anger and the slightest provocation or perceived slight from her husband caused her to be explosive. At times, even violent. Even in her workplace, Shelly reacted in anger if she didn't feel her work was properly recognized or if her ability was questioned in any way. Comparing herself with others became a huge obsession that also robbed her life of joy.

While praying together to find Shelly's release from this stronghold of emotion, one of the memories the Holy Spirit had her recall took place when she was about seven or eight years old. Shelly was participating in a school performance and was wearing an extra-special dress for the occasion. Her father had promised to come to see her perform. Because she knew he had never missed any special events that her older sister had been involved in, Shelly was certain her dad would make it to her performance and cheer her on. However, he never made it to her school that day.

When I asked her how that made her feel, I anticipated Shelly would say she had been very sad. Instead, she told me she had become very angry. In fact as she was remembering the incident, she was becoming angry thinking about it!

Me: *"Why did you feel angry?"*
Shelly: *"Because he promised and it wasn't fair."*
Me: *"Why did you think it wasn't fair?"*
Shelly: *"Because he never missed any of my sister's programs!"*

For a while Shelly was unable to explain the real reason *why* she was angry. Her anger stemmed from feeling that his "no-show" wasn't fair. He should have been there. Her father did not disappoint others – especially her older sister, with whom Shelly often compared herself with. I tried different approaches asking *why* questions, but I didn't want to put words in her mouth. So finally we sat in silence and waited for the Holy Spirit to reveal what had happened so long ago.

Soon into the silence, Shelly's tears began to fall...
Shelly: *"I didn't feel like I was worth being seen..."*
Me: *"And, how did that make you feel?"*
Shelly: *"Ugly and worthless"*

When Shelly spoke those words, the lie of the enemy became apparent and this explained *why* she reacted the way she did, not only in the original situation, but throughout her lifetime when she found herself in similar circumstances. Together we broke the power of this lie in Jesus' Name.

After the session, I had Shelly ask the Lord to speak to her heart. We waited in long silence, until tears began to fall again. She "saw" the Lord coming to her performance so long ago – the dance her earthly father had missed. The Lord Jesus spoke to her heart, "I think you are adorable" and Shelly knew it was the truth. We together found Bible passages that confirmed God's Word to her heart.

Randy, my husband will close out our stories. A few years ago Randy sensed he had hit a wall in his ministry. It was an old issue that had resurfaced. This took place just as I was beginning to grow in confidence that the Holy Spirit is the best Counselor of all! I was learning *I* didn't have to counsel people – He could do it all by Himself! The less I said, the better. What a relief for me!

Randy and I prayed together. Nothing happened. No memories. Zero, zilch, nada. Finally, after a long and uncomfortable silence, an obscure memory from childhood came to him I had never heard him talk about before.

I questioned Randy, *"How did you feel?"* Zero, zilch, nada. Randy could not remember what he felt in his emotions during the situation he was recalling. *Why do you think you didn't feel anything?* Nothing came. *Okay, let's try another memory.* A long, long silence. (Lord, where are you?). Another obscure memory. *How did that particular circumstance make you feel?* Still nothing. Again, Randy could not remember what he had felt at the time of the memory. We sat there for a very l-o-n-g time. We prayed in our spiritual languages to see if anything would break free in his soul. Nothing seemed to come to the surface. After an additional time of praying, we called it a night.

Don't ask me how a stronghold was broken in Randy's life, but from that evening forward my husband has rarely had to deal with this issue he was originally concerned about. Similar events have come into play in his life that could have tempted him to old responses. Nevertheless, Randy has been able to see through the adversary's tricks and deflect the temptation to fall into past patterns. The stronghold was broken. Mere exposure to the light of Jesus Christ broke chains we never even saw.

I could give testimony-after-glorious-testimony…

I hope that after reading these stories of others who are experiencing the freedom of the Holy Spirit in their lives, you are encouraged and excited to move forward into everything the Lord has planned for *your* life!

To Him be the glory!

---

[1] Isaiah 58:6-14, Matthew 17:21

Recommended Reading...

Waking the Dead - John Eldredge, (Nashville, TN: Thomas Nelson, Inc., 2003).

Praying God's Word - Beth Moore, (Nashville, TN: B & H Publishers, 2000).

Healing Life's Hurts - Edward M. Smith, (USA: New Creation Publishing, 2005).

Champagne for the Soul - Mike Mason, (Colorado Springs, CO: WaterBrook Press, 2003).

Captivating - John and Staci Eldredge, (Nashville, TN: Thomas Nelson, Inc., 2005).

The Conquer Series - Dr. Ted Roberts, (DVD Study, 2013).

The Bondage Breaker - Neil T. Anderson (Eugene, OR: Harvest House Publishers, 2000).

Penetrating the Darkness - Jack Hayford, (Grand Rapids, MI: Chosen, a Division of the Baker Publishing Group, 2011).

God's Cleansing Stream - Chris Hayward, (Ventura, CA: Regal Books, 2005).

Battlefield of the Mind - Joyce Meyer, (New York, NY: Faith Words, 1995).

Shame Lifter - Marilyn Hontz, (Carol Stream, IL: Tyndale House, 2009).

They Shall Expel Demons - Derek Prince, (Grand Rapids, MI: Chosen, a Division of the Baker Publishing Group, 1998, 2004).

The New Spirit Filled Life Bible **NKJV**- Jack W. Hayford, B.A., B.Th., D.D., Litt.D., Executive Editor, (Nashville, TN: Thomas Nelson, 2002).

Key Word Study Bible NIV - Spiros Zodhiates, Th.D., Executive Editor, (Chattanooga, TN: AMG Publishers, 1996).

Sue Boldt loves sharing with both small and large groups! She serves as the Pastor of Women's Ministries at Crossroads Foursquare Church in Fairfield, CA, where the love of her life, her husband Randy, is Senior Pastor. Her ministry passion is helping men and women come to know God and the freedom to be found in His love through a continually deepening relationship with Jesus. Her life's other primary joy is being mom and grandmother to her three wonderful children, their amazing spouses, and her precious grandchildren.

You can contact Sue with comments, questions or speaking engagement inquiries at susanboldt@gmail.com or at www.crossroads4you.org.

To receive daily devotionals and encouraging words, "like" the *CrossPointe with Sue Boldt Page* on Facebook! You can also "friend" her on Facebook sending a request to *Sue Cunningham Boldt.*

Please feel free to contact Sue for info on starting the *CrossPointe/CrossFire Discipleship* or *Pneuma Life* Study at your own church! Copies of CrossPointe/CrossFire may be purchased through Sue or through www.Amazon.com.

15065562R00112

Made in the USA
San Bernardino, CA
13 September 2014